Paddles On The Yukon

By

CARL T. TAYLOR

Paddles On The Yukon

1,800 Miles In A Canoe
On The Wildest River In North America

By

CARL T. TAYLOR

Illustrated
By
Mary T. Laur

Published by Mountain Empire Publications
Clifton Forge, Virginia

Paddles On The Yukon
By Carl T. Taylor

Kendrick Taylor, Editor
Illustrations and Map by Mary T. Laur
Production Assistance by Matt Laur
Photographs by Kendrick Taylor

Published by Mountain Empire Publications

Mountain Empire Publications
P.O. Box 480
Clifton Forge, VA 24422-3512

Library of Congress   98-091499
ISBN   0-9664709-0-7

This book is dedicated to all who wish to preserve the treasures of this Earth. Our stewardship on Earth lasts but a short while. May this book help prolong our stewardship by providing incentive to its readers to preserve the environment for our children and our children's children. To canoe the wildest river in North America is to experience this eternal truth that lies beyond mortality.

ACKNOWLEDGEMENTS

I am deeply indebted to Matt and Mary Laur. Mary's artistic talents added so much beauty in the book. Matt's computer production of text and reproduction of our photographs added much value and travelogue interest to the book.

My immense gratitude goes to Lee Offen, who honored us with a Foreword. His incomparable insight expressed so succinctly the essence of the book.

I count myself truly lucky to have a wife that was my bowman and editor. She put in long hours on the computer from first draft to finished script, at which point Matt took over the production work.

I must express special thanks to all the friends we met along the river that helped make our trip safe as well as pleasurable. Special friends were Betty Johnson, Alice Nerby, Mrs. Demientieff, Mr. Kallands, Pete Peteroff, John Borg, the Pitkas, the Deacons, the Freireichs, and the Flirises. I am grateful also to the many others with whom we spoke, including the Northwest Mounted Police, State Police, the storekeepers, teachers, bush pilots, and airline personnel who helped get us out of the bush.

And finally, a special word of gratitude to our family and hometown friends, who encouraged us to persevere and finish the job.

FOREWARD

Voyages of discovery are an integral part of the human condition. We take them every day. It is not often, however, that we can share someone else's voyage the way we do in reading Carl's account of his trip down the Yukon River. This is a voyage of discovery that is far more characteristic of past times in America. In earlier times, the trip would probably have been made out of necessity and not pleasure. We travel, then through time as well as Alaska and Canada with Carl and his hardy band.

This story becomes, for those of us who will never have the opportunity to make such a voyage, a chance to discover a part of America and a time unknown to us. I am grateful to Carl for giving me this opportunity. He becomes the storyteller and bard of old as he transports us in time and space to a different place with different priorities from those of 20th century "Lower 49" America.

His detailed account makes clear how different one's priorities become when in the wilderness, suddenly the concerns about bills, voicemail messages, and grocery lists are replaced with completely different things. The fireside discussion in Carl's story of "what are we carrying in our pockets," is an instructive example of how things changed for Carl and company when struggling to survive in the wilds of Alaska. It is also a chance for us all, as we read, to think about our priorities or "what is in our pockets." I will always wonder now, what is in my pockets both mental and physical and wonder why I carry what I do.

Major Lee G. Offen
U.S. Army
Arlington, Virginia

CONTENTS

Photographs

Paddles On The Yukon

PROLOGUE

Our wilderness trip started at the kitchen table with 103 topographic maps spread across its surface. The American maps were scaled 1:63,360, which meant there was one foot to every 63,360 actual feet over the land. This means that one inch on the map is one mile on the ground. The Canadian topo maps were at a 1:250,000 scale. Elevation and distance in the Rockies showed our river plunging from 2,060 feet at Lake Laberge to sea level at the Bering Sea. Racing across the Yukon Territory, it is fed by many large rivers, small streams, and glacial melt from the mountains. Near its source, it is a lively green snake, swift and wicked, and moving toward Dawson and the Alaska border, it becomes heavy with silt that changes it to a rich coffee color. But unlike coffee, it is cold, swift and deadly. These maps showed rapids, curves, hills and miles to travel. They could not show haystacks, bugs, campsites, weather and such intangibles as boredom, fatigue and danger.

We marked the more dangerous areas on the topos, and put in red our prospective camp sites for each day's travel. The strain on muscles and sinew – the subconscious effort to retain balance as one drives ash paddles into the current – is a stark reminder that life is sustained only through constant effort. Endurance is a blessing that increases with each day's work, developing abilities, independence, and skills necessary to wilderness travel. An understanding of the monotony and boredom that accompany prolonged excursions into the bush – and the interest to find challenge and education in that situation – is a skill that requires constant attention to the surroundings through which one travels.

Ken, Neill and I stopped our study of the maps to laugh about the bear that had rolled Neill and his bowman out of their tent one rainy night on the Mackenzie River. In retrospect, dangerous incidents are funny. It reminded us that we had not yet found a bowman for Neill.

Our map studies completed, and winter turning to spring, we started on the logistics of the trip. *Pollux* had been fiberglassed for our Mackenzie trip. Now it was time to fiberglass *Castor* with *Xynole*. This added about ten pounds to each boat, but kept them drier, which meant they would not increase their soak weight in the river as much.

We were faced with the problem of packing gear and equipment so that each canoe would carry a fair share. We filled a heavy black/yellow plastic bag with hammer, drill, flat and Phillips screw drivers, crescent wench, epoxy, white lead, tallow, wood screws, copper tacks, canvas strips for patching, oakum, wide flat-blade putty knife, small hand saw, chains, fish holding chains, raw hide, plastic tape, candle, and polyester putty. A collapsible tree saw and a meat saw with an extra blade were tied up under the thwarts.

We bought enough freeze-dried dinners for fifty days, expecting to find fresh and canned rations at villages along the river. Kitchen equipment was a four burner Coleman, one ice chest, an iron stew pot with a wire handle to hang over open fires, a spider and spatula, four enameled tin cups, four divided tin dinner plates, four tin place settings (spoon, fork, knife) and two large cooking spoons.

We carried two one-gallon collapsible water jugs and two one-gallon skins that would lie on top of the splash covers. Most important was our map case; that would be tied up under the forecomb of *Pollux*, in easy reach for Ken to pass maps back to me as needed.

Each crew member carried a blue nylon sea bag for personal belongings. Clothing was one change of blue jeans, shirt and underwear, three pairs of wool socks, two wool shirts, a wool winter jacket and a campaign hat to keep the rain and sun off our necks. Each person carried a slicker jacket and pants. Compasses, jackknives on belts, watches, flint, GI can openers were musts for each crewmember. Ken, as aerographer, also pocketed a wind meter, a water/air thermometer and an altimeter that measured height and distance. Ken and Neill both carried cameras. Neill stored his in an old ammo box he kept under the stern seat of his canoe, *Castor*.

Our canoes were Old Town Otcas, designed for open water canoeing. They were high combed fore and after, and each carried a deck grating. We had yellow waterproof nylon splash covers with aprons that opened at the seats to accommodate the paddlers. The covers were secured by snaps that were sewn into the hems of the covers. We screwed the bottom half of the snaps through the skin and into the oak ribs of the canoe just below the rub rail.

We made a fifteen by thirty-foot weather fly from blue rainproof nylon. We sealed the seams with spray-on waterproof cement and inserted brass grommets at the corners and the two middle seams. We then made sea bags for each member, and stenciled initials on three, leaving the yet unnamed bowman the unmarked one. Ken sewed windbreakers and pants from the same nylon for herself and me. Neill had his rain gear from other canoe trips. We gave our family members our itinerary with addresses at many of the villages where we would be stopping. Our tents were crawl-in, pop-up Jansports. They had weather flys and bug screens, with a complete cap that tied down over the inner tent. They were well designed and took less than five minutes to erect.

We carried a twelve gauge Browning shotgun, a .35 Marlin, lever action, and a .444 lever action. I left the .444 with John at Circle City for his use in the Brooks Range.

We were set to go with the exception of a missing bowman for Neill's boat, *Castor*. We had worked on faith up to this point, and apparently it worked. 6 A.M. the morning of June1st, we were ready to leave the house when our telephone rang. John's wife, Lorna, was calling to tell us her brother, Jim Smith, would like to crew for Neill. He had three attributes: young, strong and willing. We took him sight unseen, and headed for Whitehorse in our Pontiac La Mans, pulling *Castor* and *Pollux* on top of a red trailer that carried all our wilderness gear.

June 10th, and 2,793 miles later, we arrived in Dawson Creek, British Columbia. Whitehorse lay 918 miles north up the Alaska Highway. Originally called The Alcan Highway, it was built by the U.S. Engineering Corps during World War II at a cost of $140,000,000. It spans a distance of 1,524 miles from Dawson Creek to Fairbanks, Alaska.

The morning of June 16th, we crossed over the Yukon River. Below us lay history and a dangerous challenge. By mid-afternoon we were in Whitehorse. We had driven a total of ninety-five hours and five minutes.

After 918 miles on the Alaska Highway from Dawson Creek, British Columbia to the Airline Inn at Whitehorse, Yukon Territory, we arrived June 16th, covered in mud.

We drove to the international airport and found the Airline Inn, so spanking new it wasn't due to open for another week. Fortunately Don Witunik, owner, and Manfred Schuck, manager, welcomed us anyway. We became their first registered guests.

The next day John, Lorna, Barbara, their four-year-old daughter, and Jim Smith arrived. We checked for mail at the post office, then went to the Royal Canadian Mounted Police (RCMP) office, where we completed forms for wilderness travel, got our fire permit and news on the current condition of the river. The authority of the RCMP extended to Dawson.

We made plans with John and Lorna to meet us in Circle, Alaska and bring more supplies purchased in Fairbanks. The prospect of seeing family again made the thought of parting on the Yukon River tomorrow morning less sad.

The morning of departure, June 17, 1979, we left the car and trailer behind the Airport Inn at a spot Don considered safe. We also gave the keys and emergency information to him for safe-keeping. He assured us we would have rooms on our return two months from now.

At the river's edge in Rotary Park, Don offered us his river cabin to spend our first camp night. We thanked him for the thoughtfulness, but politely declined as the river was now our challenge alone. We waved goodbye to everyone, and started paddling. Don yelled, "See you someplace." Before our journey's end, we would come to understand the nuances in this uniquely Yukon farewell.

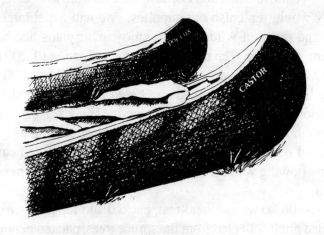

CHAPTER I
We Meet Our River

We were on the river in wind and rain. Not a good day for river travel, but to stay longer would endanger the end of our trip with cold nights and snow. The town disappeared, and the residue of civilization marred the landscape as the city dump slipped by on our left hand. Old cars, used tires, and tin cans appeared in a never-ending maze as we paddled down river. The river was fast and cold, and it was time to locate a campsite now that we were past the debris. We had covered fifteen miles of the Yukon from 10:20 to 16:20 hours. We landed, pitched the tents, and made camp. Our weather fly was spanned, and our gear well stored against further rain. Our camp, quick, rough and efficient, was comfortable and served our purpose. *Castor*, Neill's boat, developed a keel leak, the result of the bouncing it took in crossing the U.S. and traveling up the Alaska Highway. We would repair the boat in the morning.

All ties were cut to our way of life for the rest of the summer. I assumed everyone felt a twinge of melancholy, which for me stressed all too often the fact that we are alone in life, regardless of the relationships we have with each other. Well, we had another visit with John and Lorna to look forward to at Circle, where they would replenish our supplies. We had the summer before us, and miles of wilderness to enjoy. Our plans had become a living part of us. Ten months past, we had canoed 1,200 miles on the Mackenzie River. Now we looked forward to 1,800 miles of free living on the Yukon River. Freed from the shackles of civilization, we celebrated and listened. The river played noisily throughout the night, rippling along or chuckling as some roil created by current conversion or bottom obstruction caused the swift flowing water to work against itself. The day never really died.

At 06:00 we ate breakfast, packed and repaired *Castor*. We boiled pitch collected from the spruce trees, packed her hull daubing the gunk between her ribs, then painted the patch with epoxy, white lead, and tallow from our supply box. We patted the canvas back into place, sticking it to the epoxy, let it cure an hour as we cleaned the area, then packed out.

By 10:00 hours we departed Camp One on a beautiful blue river. The current swept us north toward Lake Laberge. We slipped through the old dam pile line, circa 1900, and entered into the lake at noon. The pile line is log pilings set vertically into the lake bottom with their heads bobbing at the surface of the water. This keeps the ice from building up at the head of the Yukon and causing flooding upstream.

The lake remained true to her reputation of being fraught with sudden squalls and rough seas. Thus she greeted us, only to relent and provide us with a beautiful freshet and warm sunshine for the afternoon. We canoed along the east shore of Lake Laberge for fifteen miles before making camp for our first night on the lake. We pulled *Castor* and *Pollux* through mud to dry shingle, a safe haven. The scenery was a magnificent display of mountains, mini-squalls, sun, and blue sky as seen only in arctic and subarctic regions.

We completed our camp chores, mixed a drink, and leaned against a log to enjoy wilderness peace. A rain shower chased us under our wind fly for supper at 19:00 hours. We talked of the day and watched Jim try his hand at fishing while the sun struggled toward the western horizon. The sun at this latitude and season never sets. It paused for a split second, dipped down to kiss the horizon then bounced back into the heavens. It was full light when we retired for the night to a well-earned rest and the peace of the northern wilderness.

During the night, a soft rain tapped gently on the weather shield of our tent. The wind moaned quietly in the spruce, and the freshet giggled as it bounced among the rocks that formed the streambed, lulling us into a restful sleep.

06:00 hours, the cook was up with hot coffee for the crew. The promise of a beautiful day on the river loomed before us. We packed out by 09:00 and paddled leisurely up the east shore of Laberge on a north-northeast course toward our eventual goal, the Yukon outlet known as Thirty Mile River.

One hour and ten canoe miles later, we arrived at Laurier Creek to replenish our water supply. We lingered for a short time on the creek where Jim fished for grayling, while Ken panned for gold, picking up little specks. Neill found several flecks in Laurier Creek that he quietly harvested. We returned to the boats and continued our course up Lake Laberge.

Wednesday, June 19th, showed us a kaleidoscope of pink clouds, blue sky, and purple mountain ranges to the east and west of Laberge. White wing feathers of the gulls soaring over the sage green lake blended in an ethereal way with the landscape. All was quiet and ghostly still. Our two canoes, *Castor* and *Pollux*, threaded northward. Rainsqualls added to every horizon in dynamic measure, but failed to touch our projected track line. Old Laberge treated us kindly, and we paddled on, fully enjoying the beauty, tranquility and splendor of our environment.

We made camp at 17:50 hours on an alluvial spit, pitched tents, fly sheet, and grounded the twins for the night. We tipped the canoes comb down, bracing one against the other, thus providing shelter for cargo that wasn't needed every night. Our day was done. The north end of Laberge was in view. We sat around the campfire, watched a lingering day repel darkness, and listened to the night sounds of the lake. Sleep came on quiet feet, as one by one, we crept to the comfort of our tents and a well-earned rest.

Night passed, carrying a gentle south wind with it as it moved to the north. I was speculating on the day when Ken, waking up, suggested, then requested, that I forsake my sleeping bag and make a fire. Her idea of creature comfort clashed with mine. At last, realizing that diplomacy had failed, she threatened force. Although I outweigh her by a solid one hundred pounds, I knew I was in real trouble. Reluctantly I left the tent and faced a leaden sky and light rain. The forest was wet. The world was wet. The whole of creation was soaked and Ken wanted a fire. I guessed it was up to me to build one.

Squaw wood, the small light branches of the Spruce or any conifer tree would do the trick. I broke a handful of the lower dead branches and squeezed them into a tight bundle. I covered this little bundle with small pieces of Spruce bark and a piece of pitch, then applied fire from a regular stove match from our supply, carried in a watertight plastic container. Voila! Fire!

I fed the fire with the dry wood that can be found under the wet top wood in drift piles. We soon had a hot enough blaze to consume the wet stuff with ease. Ken joined me and we warmed ourselves by the fire. Shortly after 06:00, Neill got up and the camp was astir. A pine squirrel scolded and became querulous in the nearby Spruce that had provided the squaw wood. We were on his beach and he knew it. A lone eagle fished in Laberge. We watched him swoop low over the lake, make his diving plunge and deftly grasp a white fish for his breakfast.

Slowly the weather began to change. Slower still, we began to break camp. We watched our fire die, then pushed the hot ashes into Laberge. The sun discouraged the clouds by 11:30, and we quietly departed, noting with concern the large black clouds forming to the north and west of us. We knew what they held, but trusted to luck and the Almighty as we thrust our paddles into the cold water and worked toward the northern end of Laberge and the outlet. As we neared the end of the lake, the wind began to blow and the seas rose high around us. We thanked the Lord that the wind was from our stern quarter, in that it tended to send us on our merry way with great speed. The seas grew in size, and soon began to show teeth as the tops blew over our respective freeboards and splash covers. It was a happy moment when we slipped behind a rocky bar and spotted the outlet before us. We knew we had reached the Thirty Mile section of the Yukon, and that we would soon be reasonably well sheltered from the fury of Laberge. True to the end, the Old Gal smiled, blustered, and threatened with an ever-changing mood that, within a matter of minutes, either spelled tranquility or threatened disaster. She let us go in peace.

CHAPTER II
Down North

The Thirty Mile River section was an extremely fast and beautiful part of the Yukon River. Entering Thirty Mile, we spotted the bones of the old riverboat *Casca I* on our right hand. There she lay, rotting and in total disrepair. I thought of the *Cremation of Sam McGee*, and wondered if Robert Service had known of the Casca and used it as a setting for his poem.

"Since I left Plumtree down in Tennessee, this is the first time I've been warm,"

as the poem goes. Neill and Ken could already identify with Sam. Our weather was staying in the fifties and low sixties, requiring warm clothing to stay comfortable.

The river, blue-green and swift, sped us past the remains of the old steamer and my thoughts were soon forgotten. We were sheltered from the open waters of Lake Laberge and the wild confusion of the tumbling waves that had shoved us into this beautiful stretch of water. Even so, it was evident that we all had to keep a sharp watch on the river and the current as it roiled and rolled under our keels and before us.

Thirty Mile is 150 feet wide, racing between perpendicular sand and gravel bluffs of two to three hundred feet in height above the river's surface. We were moving at great speed in the grip of this river. We found ourselves doing wheelies around the bends, calling for each canoer to be alert. The bends in the river were especially shallow, and expert sternmen were needed to keep the canoes from scraping off paint and canvas. This was no place for a novice to learn to read water. Lake Laberge had been kindergarten for us.

We soon spotted a fine campsite and beached our boats, knowing full well we were now committed to the Yukon and all that it could bring. Our camp was ideal, providing fresh fish for Jim, who is an avid fisherman, and beautiful serene vistas for all to enjoy. The half-light of night and the outstanding topography soon lulled us to sleep as the river provided music found only in the wilderness.

Morning came on quiet feet, producing a beautiful day. Jim caught grayling and whitefish, which we ate for breakfast. We packed our gear and moved on. The Yukon proved interesting – fast water raced over rocks and a cobbled bed, giving the bowmen in both *Castor* and *Pollux* plenty of excitement. Riffles in several areas added to the excitement, and one outstanding curve known as U.S. Bend added to the danger and grandeur of the landscape.

A canoe manned by Carol and Randel, two young teachers enroute to a teaching job in western Alaska, rushed past us. On our way to Hootalinqua, we were entertained by the wildlife. Our canoes slipped past a cow moose with her calf, a beaver came up under my paddle and got a paddle on the rear end for his troubles. Two otters played along side our canoes, diving and surfacing in contra temp, and muskrats riffled the grasses along the shoreline. Waterfowl taking off in front of our canoes were Old Squaws, Mallards, Teal, and a pair of early Great Northern Loons. The mountain weather remained fickle; hot sun at midday and a drenching rain by 14:00 hours, followed by a pelting of heavy hail. We reached the confluence of the Yukon and Teslin rivers and Balmoral by 17:00. We arrived at Chateau Balmoral, on the site of the Hootalinqua overnight camping area. We found Carol and Randel already camped for the night.

Balmoral was a log cabin built in the thirties by an old timer named Andy Johnson, who bar mined on the Teslin River. He and his nephew, Bob Jones, used the site until 1955. The Water Survey of Canada bought the property. In an effort to perpetuate the ways of the north, the company left an open and standing invitation to use the cabin as shelter. River travelers often do, although we camped in the rain about seventy-five yards south of the structure. The cabin was in disrepair, but Hootalinqua was the only stop where we found strongly built and well kept out-houses. Only the marmots could peek under the door.

Night at Hootalinqua was far from quiet. Hootalinqua, in Athabascan, means the meeting or joining of the waters. It was the joining of the waters of the Teslin and Yukon that brought the arrival of fellow travelers, several by canoes, others by powerboats. They were from Whitehorse, and on vacation. We listened as they pitched camp at the sight of the old roadhouse, and finally heard them settle for the night. Following a quick evening meal, we retired while Jim, an ever eager fisherman, fished. It rained.

By 06:00, the twilight of the night was rapidly losing its battle with the gray overcast of the day. Wisps of fog floated on a light breeze and fine rain fell. We crawled out of our tents, and with a joint effort, browbeat a fire into signs of life. Ken made break-fast and was assisted by a small marmot who readily ate cereal from a spoon. We ate our cereal and waited for the weather to clear. The weather set the cadence for the day, as we never packed out wet.

I left camp and walked to Balmoral to sit on a bolt of stove wood by an old table used for many things: eating, carpentry, cleaning game and guns, or whatever. For me it was a desk. The one window in Balmoral provided light. The log structure, ten by ten feet, had little in the way of headroom. It was reasonably dry, providing shelter from the rain and weather if one stood away from the holes in the roof. Its guest book gave ample testimony of the log cabin's usefulness. It was a safe haven, used by many traveling the Yukon and Teslin Rivers enroute to God knows where in the Yukon. The little marmots tried to lay claim to this structure also, only to be disturbed by man. They were bold and determined, and with a little luck may one day lay complete claim to Balmoral.

Around 09:30, the weather cleared. We started to break camp, but our things – all things – were wet. The boats were filled in their after-ends with rainwater. Clothes and food bags needed sun, and we needed a bath. By 11:00, the weather was clear. We needed a day out of the boats. All were in agreement. We loafed.

Throughout the day the weather played games. First we had sun. We bathed. It rained. We washed clothes. It rained. So the day went. Ken's marmot grew quite tame. Ken tried to write. The marmot attempted to get on her lap. Finally, she put the cheese away and solved part of the problem. After all, Hootalinqua belonged to all creatures, mostly the marmots.

Mid-afternoon, we reviewed the maps. Names such as Mistake, Surprise, The Dome, Poroas and Lewes Mountains – by now familiar – would in all probability never be seen again, and yet we four had experienced their grandeur and could call them by name. Thirty Mile River, which yesterday surged us northward, pelting us with rain and hail, was today a mere line on the 1:250,000 scale map we tucked away in our map case. So a river trip goes, and so ours would continue. Tomorrow we would canoe north and west toward Alaska.

The morning of June 23rd broke clear with a blue sky and sun. It was a great day for travel. Ken popped from the tent at 05:30 and made breakfast. We packed the canoes and prepared to leave Hootalinqua. As we did, we noticed two other powerboats had arrived during the night. The owners told Jim they were from Whitehorse and bound for Dawson. For these Canadians, Whitehorse to Dawson was a terrific two week summer vacation, which they considered a real life Disney World experience.

This explained the well-built outhouses. They loaded their boats with plenty of food and drink and good books, and let the mighty Yukon do the work for them as they floated the majority of the way to Dawson, through a majestic wilderness sans plastic and Styrofoam.

We readied our two boats for the river, and at 08:30 hours we were underway. We cleared a bad spot in the river by dint of hard paddling, especially by the bowmen. Thinking as we paddled that a motor would provide help we picked up a strong current from the Teslin River that shot us to midstream. We were making good time, and we marked our progress by watching the high mud and clay banks slide past. A small island appeared on our left hand, where we saw the remains of an old river steamer, a relic from the gold rush of '89. She sat high and dry on the island. She was named *Evelyn*. Little else was known of her career on the river, if, indeed, she ever worked on the Yukon. She lies as proof that history, even in the making, is fast fading and soon lost in the changing panorama of time.

The hours wore on as the shore slipped by. We paddled past Klondike Bend and Big Salmon. Our maps showed Big Salmon as an abandoned Indian village located at the mouth of the Big Salmon River. It earned its name from the size of the fish that at one time were caught there. As we continued on down the Yukon, we looked for, but could not find, Byer's wood camp. From all indications, both time and erosion had wiped Byer's camp from the river, or we missed it. Nearing Freeman's Rock below Big Salmon, we spotted an old gold dredge on the Right Bank. It was constructed about 1940, but never used. It remains mute testimony to the fickleness that accompanies gold fever.

We entered a small clear water slip to escape the strong pressure of a headwind that had plagued us during the morning hours. Putting out long lines to secure the canoes so we could stretch and eat lunch, Ken perfected her unique method of debarking from the canoe. Disembarking up a steep bank, Ken reached for a twig to assist her. It was dead and gave way. Sitting in the stern of *Pollux* I saw her plunging stern first down the bank toward the port gunwale and the ice cold water of the stream. I leaned far out to starboard knowing we were in for a quick swim. I felt the shock as Ken's foot hit the gunwale. The boat shook, righted its self, and as I looked, a grinning Ken was scrambling up the bank. She was dry and so was I. I will never know how this maneuver was accomplished, and Ken won't talk.

As we ate lunch, our Whitehorse motorboat friends drifted by on the current. They were leaning back in comfortable chairs reading books while the Yukon did the work for them. We hailed each other as they passed. Ken said we looked like greenhorns working our butts off paddling against headwinds and cross currents, only to be passed by these merry current drifters every time we stopped for lunch, water, or the evening's camp. We lay exhausted. They reclined in their boats and laughed. Like the citizens of St. Ignace, who called their summer tourists *Fudgies* because they were the only ones who ate their famous fudge candy, these current drifters probably had a name for us. Ken suggested *current cowboys*, but we never asked.

After six and a half hours of canoeing down river amidst sun, squalls and headwinds, we located a good spot on a small dry island. We pulled the canoes, pitched camp, ate a freeze-dried stroganoff supper, and retired.

Sunday June 24th at 05:30, we ate a leisurely breakfast, packed in a slow, steady manner, and launched our canoes at 09:00 hours. We passed Columbia Rock, Little Salmon, and Eagle Rock, jagged metamorphic rock outcroppings on the right hand rising seven hundred feet above the river. We knew from our maps that we were in the vicinity of Carmacks, where we could replenish supplies. We needed food, hardware, and a fifth of Canadian Club – the last of which we could buy for an enormous price. The prospect of adding to our supplies put us in good humor.

Our intent, as we launched our canoes, was to make camp near Carmacks and enter the town early Monday morning. The river, weather, and wind worked with us most of the day. In the afternoon we had small squalls, nothing serious. We also had headwinds, but when one elects to canoe 1,800 miles in a land known as the "home of the winds," what can one expect?

During the day we refilled our water skins with fresh drinking water at Claire Creek, a beautiful glacial stream running into the muddy Yukon. We stopped briefly at Little Salmon, another abandoned Indian village. Big Salmon and Little Salmon were sad places to visit, with grave markers and spirit houses now paying tribute to a small pox epidemic that wiped out the community in the early 1800's.

A strong south wind added enough momentum to our paddling for a fast fifty mile day on the river. We ran *Pollux* over a gravel bar, fortunately with little damage. We were tired. We pitched our tents on a small spindrift, no name island near Carmacks. We pulled our canoes high, leaving their sterns near the water, then placed a marker stick at the water's edge to keep track of the water level in the river. It is a good habit for all river travelers, in that it is always safer to know the level and type of water you are running. Such information assists you in making the right decision for safe passage.

The evening meal was fish we had caught while at Claire Creek. Jim toured the island on foot. Neill wrote letters home. Ken retired to the tent, and I settled to bringing my log up to date.

Monday brought in a windy morning. We checked our stick, placed last evening at water level between *Castor* and *Pollux*. It indicated a two inch rise in the level of the river. That meant lots of water through Five Finger Rapids. We face the slot Tuesday. We ate a quick breakfast at 05:45 hours, and said farewell to our little spindrift island haven. We faced the usual Yukon, with its strong headwinds and sweepers.

We made two landings for Carmacks, the first well above the Carmacks Bridge because of an indication of logjams and hangers on the bridge abutment. We landed and walked to a high spot of ground from which we could see the cause. Tree trunks and broken limbs were hung up on the left bank abutments, acting as bobbers and deadmen spewing great fountains of water by obstructing the current. From this vantage point, we selected an approach to the bridge itself and a channel through which we could avoid these obstructions. We returned to our boats, ran the gauntlet, and landed at the ramp below the bridge in style. We reached Carmacks at 11:30, left Jim to watch the boats, and made our trek to town.

Carmacks was named after George Washington Carmacks, who discovered gold and coal mines there in 1896. The mines have been in operation since the turn of the century. In more recent times, the coal was used for drying concentrates of silver, lead and zinc, byproducts of mining gold. This mining provides a good living for the village of Carmacks and its 225 inhabitants. The steel bridge spanning the Yukon at Carmacks is part of the road system connecting Dawson City with Whitehorse and civilization.

Upon reaching the town of two dozen homes and buildings, we shopped for groceries, visited the RCMP (no one home, out on patrol), and purchased a map from the Forest Service. We hit a licensed lounge for a few beers and the real privilege of sitting in chairs. Ken called home on the radio telephone. It was Jim's turn to visit town. He learned that a young grizzly had been shot near Carmacks on the 23rd of June, that a large grizzly had been tranquilized and moved to a far location, and that a woman had been mauled near Whitehorse by yet another grizzly. All this bear activity was attributed to the fact the river was very high, making it difficult for the bear to catch their share of salmon. The bear have to eat, people sleep in their domain, and people are protein.

Jim returned to the landing with his purchases, mostly peanut butter, which we helped him eat. We departed Carmacks at 14:50 hours, bound for Five Finger Rapids. We knew the Yukon River was high, campsites hard to locate, the wind heavy at times, and drinking water scarce. We needed a good site to overnight before taking on the rapids, so when Ken spotted an old fish camp we hove to at 16:00. It was high up the right bank in a clump of spruce trees. We pulled the boats, pitched camp, and before retiring, reviewed our map of the rapids area. High water meant bad rapids. Voices below our high camp told us we had caught up with our Whitehorse vacationers. They were also waiting for morning to run the rapids.

Before sleep closed my day I thought not of danger, or possible death from heart stopping ice cold water, or the morrow, or Five Finger and later Rink Rapids. I thought of our crew and how each in his or her own way psychologically prepared for what would be our coming attraction. Why the question? For what reason? How would each respond when faced with possible haystacks, roosters, growlers and the final pitch and thunder of the rapids? I fell into a fitful sleep. My questions went unanswered.

CHAPTER III
Rapids and History

Morning came with a cold wind and the promise of rain. We were up by 05:45, and ate a quick breakfast in preparation for running the rapids. We divided the provisions; supplies and clothing evenly, then packed each half in the canoes. This way, should one of the canoes be capsized or swamped, we would have enough gear to get us safely to the next village. We packed the provisions in the center of the boats. We snapped the splash covers into place along the center section between the spreaders, with the ends of the covers – that ordinarily kept the occupants dry – packed under and around the provisions, then tightly lashed in place. This arrangement would prevent any chance of someone getting tangled in the splash covers should there be an accident.

We double-checked the ties on the rifles and the extra paddles strapped along the bow and stern of the canoes and made fast to the gunwales. We checked our map case and pulled the Velcro tightly around them. We forced the case into the bow of the canoe under the forecomb deck as far as possible. Then we lashed the case in place through the limber holes between the ribs and the grab rail. We added grab lines to both sides of the canoes by the stern and bow seats. Our work, completed to our satisfaction, now allowed the twins, *Castor* and *Pollux*, complete independence should one be lost.

Talk was scarce as we prepared ourselves for running the rapids. We heard the Whitehorse Gang (as we had nicknamed them), depart before us. We wanted to give them plenty of time to clear the rapids before we had to go down the slot.

An hour down stream, we passed the ruins of the Northwest Mounted Police Five Finger Detachment Outpost. We knew the rapids would soon come into view. We could hear the roar of the water as it shouldered its way through the basalt barricade, raging at the world for toying with its progress. The sound of our paddles in military cadence, the sighing wind, the driving rain on splash covers and rain slickers added ominous noises to the hissing current that tore at the bank. A Bull Moose with lichen hanging on his trophy size rack stood knee deep in the river quietly watching our passage. *Castor* and *Pollux* danced heel to toe toward the maelstrom.

We made a sharp right angle turn along the right limit of the river. The rapids and falls came sharply into view. Before us stood the four fifty-foot basalt towers like sentinels, forcing the river to break into five passages, only to come together on the downside in fantastic disarray.

It was time for each of us to kneel on the floor grating and brace our upper legs against the ribbing and gunwale. We stayed to the right limit. We saw the "V" the conflicting currents made between the bank and the first basalt turret. We hit the "V" that plunged us into rollers topping the forecomb. The swirling mass of water sent *Pollux* hurtling into the main body of the rapids and falls.

Our canoe bobbed, dipped, submerged, rose and dipped again making the water break square in Ken's face. The bow stood too high for her to paddle. It was up to me to hold the canoe on course as we fought our way through the deranged torrent.

At keel level, the water, growling and snarling, fought with us through the outer barrier of swells and into the maw of rock ledges, giant stair steps, dropping us in successive twelve and eighteen foot falls to the lowest level of the river. The bowmen took the brunt of the haystacks and roosters breaking against the high comb, and the canoes shipped water as we knifed through the turbulence.

Wet and cold and scared, we won. Close on our starboard hand, *Castor* proudly shot clear on her tack. We did a high port salute to each other.

We suddenly became aware of a motor boat stranded on a small green island in the midst of the turmoil. They were waving and shouting at us to attract our attention. It was our Whitehorse Gang who had been thrown up on the beach. We were traveling too fast to stop along side them and there was no stopping along the banks without breaking up the hulls of our canoes.

"We'll see you in Dawson," they yelled, letting us know they did not need help.

Half-hour later we shot past Tatchum Creek and found solid ground on the right bank of the Yukon, where we could make a safe landing. We were wet and cold and in need of a break. We built a fire, dried our clothes and our nerves and ate a quick lunch. We turned the canoes on their sides to drain out the shipped water before re-embarking to meet our second challenge of the day, Rink Rapids, a scant six miles north.

The channel rocks, which once made Rink Rapids the scourge of the Yukon, had been removed by the Canadian government to make the river safer for travel. However, bits and broken parts of ships sunk there still littered the bottom with rudders, boilers and iron trappings from old side-wheelers. Although there were no falls on these rapids, the outjutting rock formations still made it dangerous passage for canoes and small crafts.

The river seemed intent on pushing vessels against the rock formations. Through rapids like Rink bowmen are indispensable. They keep the bow going straight down the slot and when necessary push the bow and forequarters away from rocks and submerged objects, giving the sternmen the needed space to maneuver the canoe down the "V" of the turbulent current. It was

Rink in the rain for us. We might have called Rink an anti-climax, except we were again cold and wet and wishing for a quiet, warm camp.

We left the river at Yukon Crossing, which had been an important way station during the gold rush years. The trip ran from Whitehorse to Dawson City and back, carrying men and supplies for the gold camps. It was equipped with a ferry for summer travel, and used by the stagecoaches during the winter when they could cross on the ice. The abandoned log roadhouse, deteriorating log cabins, sod-roofed barn and blacksmith shop still stood as testimony to its past importance.

The main room of the roadhouse was covered with Louis XIV rococo blue flocked wallpaper. The log walls had been pasted with linen upon which the wallpaper was pasted for an elegant appearance, suited for gentlemen of leisure or scam. We found it a good place to camp. We set our tents on flat ground covered with deep green grass. Carol and Randel, whom we met at Hootalinqua had already made camp near by.

Prior to retiring for the night, we pulled *Castor* and *Pollux* into Crossing Creek, emptied them of cargo, and gave them a much needed bucket bath to rid them of our old shipmate, Mud, which seems to find its way into all boats traveling the Yukon. An old bachelor beaver swam in Crossing Creek and slapped his tail on the water as both a warning to fellow forest creatures, and an expression of irritation at our presence in his domain. We heard him throughout the night. Still, we enjoyed a good night's sleep as fear, fatigue and cold melted away in the warm tent.

Our night passed without incident. It rained off and on during the gray of night but quit before we were up at 05:40. After breakfast with camp chores done, *Castor* and *Pollux* were floated and packed. By 10:00, we were in Crossing Creek taking fresh drinking water aboard. At the confluence of the creek and the Yukon, we paddled into the swift strong current.

We passed the abandoned town of Minto, or so our map said, only to find it re-inhabited. Minto had been a trading post and stopping place for river steamers. Nothing remained of the old buildings, but several new log cabins could be seen from the river. We made camp forty miles down river on a sand-washed island after six hours of paddling.

We collected wood for our evening fire and had a round of drinks, our last until Dawson. We were discussing the latest information on grizzly attacks when it occurred to us we had not fired either the .35 caliber or the .444 rifles. Jim had little experience with guns and the rest of us figured we could stand some familiarization and drill. We considered it prudent to do so, because of bear sign and wolf tracks in the shingle and along the beach. Fire we did, and I was pleased to note that Jim shot well enough to hit our target. At 21:00 hours we retired, aware of the rising wind. Tomorrow could see us weather bound, otherwise we would head for Fort Selkirk, which was also marked abandoned on the maps.

Breaking camp on June 28th, we entered the Yukon with a following east wind that had blown hard all night. We cleared our island, and with our backs as sails, hit a strong current and made rapid progress down stream. Thank goodness we were not attempting to breast that current or make progress against it. We ate up the miles, and by 12:30 we were on the beach at Fort Selkirk.

Fort Selkirk, with the Anglican Church in the center of town. The sign inside the church read, "You are 1,520 miles from the Bering Sea. How far are you from God?"

Fort Selkirk was established in 1848 by Robert Campbell of the Chilkoot and Chilkat tribes. Its original location at the mouth of the Pelly River was subject to flooding. It was moved to its present site as a result, and was ransacked by Indians in 1852. It was never again put back in operation. We visited the ruins, all log and in general disrepair. We stopped by the Anglican Church that was established by Bishop Bompas, and now being maintained by the Episcopal Mission. We read several posted messages written by church members visiting the site during float trips to Dawson, and sometimes answered by fellow travelers. One message read: "You are 1,520 miles from the mouth of the Yukon River on the Bering Sea. How far are you from God?" We pondered the question for a brief moment and wrote our answer. "We are one freeboard away."

Neill, Jim, and I waited while Ken collected wild flowers for her book, which was becoming quite a volume. Neill took pictures of us standing in front of the Taylor & Drewery general store. We departed.

We passed the Pelly River on the right hand. Her headwaters start in the glacial lakes of the Pelly Mountain. She adds a cold current to the Yukon, increasing its already swift current. Victoria Rock stands high and proud at 2,900 feet on our left. It was given to Queen Victoria by the Canadian Government in celebration of the turn of the century in 1900. She died at 83 years of age in 1901 after a 68 year reign over the British Empire.

At 15:00 hours, we began the search for a campsite. The wind remained strong. We probed islands and streams and scanned the swiftly passing shoreline. It was the usual problem – bad banks, too high, no place for canoes, or too dangerous to attempt a landing, etcetera. Three hours later, we landed on a small spindrift island amid bugs, mud, and black alders. It was home. We pulled the boats, pitched the tents, collected wood for our fire, drank Russian tea, ate, drank coffee, and read our maps. It was exactly fifty miles down the Yukon from breakfast. Satisfied, we crawled into our tents, out of the wind, to rest.

During the night we awoke in the midst of a cathedral-like silence. The wind had died. This quietness lasted throughout the morning. We experienced sun and no wind, which had grown tired of blowing, I suppose. It was heaven. The river of last evening, strong, loud and full of mischief, was at peace. The current still raced, but the fury was not as evident. We ate in silence and sunlight, and at 09:00 hours we departed.

Within the hour the Yukon grew broad and sullen. We changed charts from Carmacks to Snag. The name took on an ominous note, boding evil. We stayed alert. Hours wore on. Cripple Creek, Selwyn, Isaac Creek, once names on our maps, then real places, then names again as we canoed past them.

Britannia Creek, a small stream that falls from the Canadian Rockies, hosts a placer gold mine. C. Guxe flies a small chopper from this operation. We spoke with two men working on the engine of the chopper as we passed, giving them answers to the questions asked by other people we had met on the river. "Where did you put in?" And, "Where are you bound?" "Where do you call home?" "Whitehorse." "Russian Mission." "Maryland, Virginia, Florida and California," in that order.

Five miles north-northwest of Britannia Creek, we located a small island with a dry headland. It looked good enough to pitch our weather fly and wait out the coming rain. We stood under the fly and drank hot tea as an easterly wind pelted us with cold drops of rain. We were happy to be off the Yukon for a short time and sheltered from the weather. Not wanting to face more rain on the river, we pitched our tents for the night. One by one we slipped into our tents. Under the blue nylon dome, out of the wind and rain, we were warm and dry. Ken wrote letters home and I read *The Mad Trapper* by Dick North. Sleep stole the final scene.

03:00 hours on the morning of June 30th, I awakened to a gray, fog filled morning. The wind was still. No rain. I became aware of the air pump on the Coleman stove. Jim was heating water for coffee. He had started the morning fire. At 04:00, Ken's head appeared from her sleeping bag, asking the usual question relating to time. Her ten dollar pocket watch, purchased in Whitehorse, never worked at night. When she received the answer she got up. Day began. We drank coffee by the fire, ate Red River Cereal, a five-grain mixture, and talked about the river. Slowly we packed. Things were nearly ready when the usual thing happened. It rained. The small white cloud of fog remained glued to the mountainside, and rain on cats' paws crept slowly up the Yukon. It pounced on us. We heaped wood on our dying fire and stood under our fly sheet watching and waiting for a break in the weather. At 09:00 hours the weather moderated. We boarded *Castor* and *Pollux* and paddled north and west down river.

More names and places were passed and committed to memory: Coffee Creek, a beautiful blackwater river, Halfway Creek, and Independence Creek – more blackwater with bear sign. Kirkman Creek was inhabited by a small band of Crow Indians. Los Angeles Creek and Thistle Creek came next in sight, as did a large dark storm. We crossed the Yukon to the west bank and rigged our weather fly. It rained and pelted us with hail. Within the hour, however, Ken and Neill spotted a rainbow on East Mountain. We packed our weather sheet in wet boats and made for the spot of sunshine that illuminated a sand spit on a no name island. Camp chores and supper ended our long wet day, as did the sunshine that warmed us at long last.

Sunday July 1st, we awakened at 06:30 hours. I started a fire with Neill's help. We had coffee compliments of Jim. Ken crawled from the tent and started breakfast. Pancakes and reconstituted eggs.

The day started with sun. By 10:00 it threatened rain and produced hordes of mosquitoes. I took a bucket bath and crawled into the tent to read. Jim fished. No luck. Neill was off in search of firewood. He returned with a question relating to a hen grouse and her chicks who had vanished before his eyes. I told him the hen went for cover and the chicks had covered themselves with leaves leaving no evidence of ever having been there. Ken read. We all loafed. After all, it was Sunday, and Dawson was only one hundred miles away.

The lazy day drifted by. We washed clothes. The sun was hot. In the afternoon we picked tiny flecks of gold from the sand in front of the tents. The total pleasure of doing nothing in the immense stillness of the subarctic, under the boundless blue sky filled with sunshine, was beyond verbal description. The day needed an artist.

At 19:00 hours, we ate a quick freeze-dried spaghetti supper. The wind howled, making the tents shake like living things in the extreme fatigue of a high fever. It rained buckets, then, like the chicks, vanished as the winds abated and the area became virginal. A beautiful rainbow appeared in the northeast. We four blessed the day and retired to our tents, thankful to be warm and dry.

On July 2nd, our 15th day on the river, I awakened at 04:30 hours, opened the tent fly, and watched as the elements tussled for control of the day. A gray, black, and blue sky let narrow shafts of sunlight reach the mountains as black clouds rolled over them, allowing rain to fall freely to a hardly parched earth. All things were wet, and small traces of fog floated through the spruce and conifers. The wind whispered in the black alders along the Yukon at low level, while high above the tumbling clouds gave ample testimony to the wildness of high altitude weather. Finally the sun won a hand. The camp stirred. Jim and Neill were up. I left the tent at Ken's urging, and helped Neill with the camp chores. The Coleman stove sprang to life and wood was gathered for our morning fire, which we started from a small piece of birch bark carried for such purposes. The bark, peeled very thin, readily ignites when a match is applied to it. It has a good deal of oil, and will burn in any type of weather long enough to ignite squaw wood that, in turn, will cause heavy pieces of wood to eventually burn. Bark of the birch tree can be found in the north, and is easily stripped from broken or rotting logs. Peeled and rolled in small bundles, it can be stored in the comb of canoes and is a real lifesaver when quick fires are needed.

Soon Ken was up and breakfast was prepared. We ate in silence, listening to the river and the squall of a moose calf who had temporarily lost its mother on the east bank of the Yukon. Suddenly the racket ceased. The little fellow was secure once more.

At 08:20 we left our snug harbor and paddled north down river. During the day, we crossed the confluence of the White River and Frisco Creek. Mount Stewart, at 4,000 feet, loomed over us from the east. The Stewart River came into view and quickly slid by to starboard, as did Burian's store, the only occupied establishment at Stewart River. We did not stop. Shamrock Dome, 3,000 feet high, watched our progress from the port hand.

The weather took many turns – sun, wind, rain, and more rain. Gray and black clouds sailed around us. The wind slowly became a headwind as we worked our way down north. At 14:30 hours we had had enough. We spotted, liked, and claimed a small island for our own. The camp was pitched and tea time was called. Shortly thereafter, Ken went to the tent. Her notes required attention. Jim worked on his belt knife, and Neill watched a beaver slide for signs of activity. I watched the storm clouds to the west until Ken joined us under the fly to start supper.

We ate an evening meal that consisted of bannock, mulligan, and hot coffee. Neill gave the pots a Murphy scrub with creek sand. Our fire did the drying and sterilizing. We put a nice bow on the day and filed it away in memory. Just before sleep closed my eyes, I thought, "Thirty-nine miles to Dawson."

On July 3rd, a large orange ball appeared in the east. The illumination inside the tent was a thing of beauty. I crawled to the door for a view of the sky. Wonderful! It was clear. No clouds were visible. Somehow, the heavens had purged themselves and were for the most part pure. How long would this beautiful sunshine last? By the time I located my gear and put myself together, Neill, who was up doing his sun dance, had a smudge going. Ken, also a sun worshiper, was soon up and absolutely on top of the morning. I helped her with the Coleman. It was coffee time.

Within a short time, Ken began to get too warm. The arctic sun grew too hot for undershirt, shirt, overshirt and coat. The conversation centered on Dawson. When should we arrive? What do we really require in the way of supplies? Time held the answer and time would be measured by paddles and applied effort. We ate breakfast and departed at 09:00 hours. Rose Butte and Lucky Joe Creek passed by, as did many small, unnamed islands. The current ran fair and foul as we canoed back and forth across the river searching for the fastest passage. Reindeer Mountain to the east and Tyrrell Mountain to the northwest – then west, and finally west-southwest – monitored our passage.

At noon, we stopped on a small gravel spit for a quick lunch. Twenty-five minutes later we were again at the paddles. We needed fresh water and vainly searched the west bank for a small clear stream or spring. It was on one of these casts that we spotted two moose. We saw three beautiful whistling swans, which Ken photographed with our Bino-camera.

16:20 hours we crossed the Yukon to the east bank – a distance of five hundred yards of seething current – and found what might have been Eisley Creek, an old Indian fishing camp, and good water. We also saw, panned, and captured several small flecks of red gold. It was during this stop that Ken fell in the creek, found gold, and spotted what might have been the Old Garner Creek mine high on a mountain to the north. She was having a busy day. We left the creek mouth and paddled north to a small island. We had been in the canoes for eight hours and twenty-five minutes. It was time to call it a day.

As we pulled our boats from the river, we noticed visitors. An organization known as Gold Rush 05 rents aluminum canoes to people interested in floating the Yukon from Whitehorse to Dawson at a cost of $150 per week. Our visitors, three in number, were busy crossing the river in our direction. They hit the shingle with a crash that sounded like rocks being rolled in an oil drum. It made us fear for the canoe. One young chap came up the bank toward us and asked the distance to Dawson. We told him by our reckoning it was thirty-nine miles. He departed with his three-canoe flotilla, streaming his canoe incorrectly, and causing us to wonder at the wisdom of sending greenhorns onto the Yukon with as little experience as he appeared to possess. Tomorrow we will be in Dawson.

We turned our attention to eating supper. A freeze-dried concoction under the practiced hand of Ken always tasted excellent, but Ken said it was not her hand; it was the hand of hunger that added the gourmet flavor.

The sun, that subarctic and arctic monster that never sleeps at this season of the year, finally disappeared behind a mountain. It was time for all to rest. The cooling night breezes soon saw to that as they seemed to whisper, "Dawson tomorrow then on down north to Alaska on a swift flowing Yukon."

I awoke to the realization it was Independence Day. At 05:00, the sun was high, but the night's chill still lingered. I left the tent and started a fire. Neill was up. Ken crawled from our tent and gazed in amazement at the day as she warmed herself by the fire. Jim joined us in time for breakfast, coffee, and pack out.

I was walking toward the river when I spotted a cow moose

and calf swimming mid-stream in a strong current. I called for all to see. The cow, attracted by my voice, raised herself high in the water to better locate the source of my voice. Once she located me she breasted the current to protect her calf and started the long cold swim to the west bank from where she came. Ken and Neill took pictures and watched as both animals disappeared down river. We then returned to packing and the business of getting things ready for Dawson and an Independence Day drink in a gold rush bar.

CHAPTER IV
Dawson to Alaska

We landed below the Canadian Bank of Commerce in Dawson at 10:00. We walked through Dawson, checked in with the RCMP, who wished us well on the remainder of our journey, shopped for food, and mailed letters home. We visited the bank, where they showed us several nuggets of gold. "How do you keep people from snitching all these nuggets laid out on the table like that?" Ken asked. The lady showing us around and telling us the history of the gold rush told us to pick one up.

The small one was a gold washed raisin and the large one a prune. Everyone had a good laugh and Ken conned the lady out of a raisin nugget.

We walked around town. It was being rebuilt in the 1898-1902 goldrush style. We ate lunch at the El Dorado and had a beer in their Sluice Lounge. At the bar, we found out the miners were selling their nuggets directly to the jewelers who paid them on average $1,200 an ounce, as opposed to the banker who offered $200 - $400, depending on the quality of the gold. The bankers could tell from which gold site the nuggets came. The original Rabbit Creek gold was red gold, still the best quality.

We went to the Nuggets and Things Shop and bought souvenirs to take home.

Our Whitehorse Gang ended their summer vacation here and started for home. No longer able to float on the current, their motor boats would be working hard to get them back to Whitehorse. Turning to practical business, we went to a small store near the landing and bought postcards to send home and a pocketknife to replace the one lost in the river. Heading for our canoes, we passed a fake paddlewheeler, the "Yukon Lou," tied up at the dock and blasting out Robert Service Yukon poems set to music. It was waiting for the tourists to board for a 10 mile trip down the canyon and back to Dawson. The canyon is a narrow stretch of the Yukon that causes ice, during the spring break-up, to jam along the high banks, leaving the water no place to go but into the streets and houses of Dawson. The water was still high, giving us a swift ride down stream through the canyon to Fort Reliance.

At Fort Reliance, we found a small island and decided to camp for the night. The island was directly across the river from Fort Reliance, which had been a military garrison from the gold rush days through World War II. We were not happy with this camp because of mud, garbage and crud washed down from Dawson. This attracted a profusion of black flies, gnats, and no-see-ums.

Standing around the evening campfire, we all agreed we would move out early in the morning. Tomorrow, weather permitting, we would push on toward the great State of Alaska. Our day was done 'neath the midnight sun'.

Before sleep closed my eyes, I gave Ken a token gift in honor of our third anniversary. It was a small gold pan made from a Yukon nugget. On the bottom of the pan in script letters was the word "Dawson." Ken hadn't seen me buy it and was really surprised.

July 5th was dull, gray, and quiet in the early hours. By 05:30, Ken and I had packed our gear. 06:00 hours Neill appeared and joined us for hot coffee. Jim showed up at 07:00

following a poke from Neill. We ate breakfast and entered the river by 08:20.

We moved downstream past the lower end of the old fort and talked of what lay before us. We remembered a RCMP officer said: "If you found the trip from Whitehorse to Dawson a wild and lonely experience, the next two hundred miles to Circle would make the initial run look like Main Street on a busy shopping night. Travelers on this section of the river would be few, and stopping places farther apart and difficult to locate." We thanked him for the "good" news; after all, it was a wilderness trip that we wanted to take.

We passed Moosehide, a small Indian village on the right bank. Most of the families that once lived there had moved to Dawson or elsewhere, leaving the cabins, church and schoolhouse to the weather. The few remaining families were busy getting fish wheels ready for the salmon run, which had just begun to appear in that section of the Yukon River.

The day remained overcast and promised rain, which the clouds delivered along with stiff headwinds. We bucked the wind for a good two hours and finally sought a lea. The day dissolved around us. We rested for a brief period then left our snug harbor, rounded a point, and ran again into the wind and rain. We made for the west bank, where we beached our canoes and built, American-like, a big, hot, fire. The bank was steep and rocky, but provided a grand view of the river. Several outboards passed by on their way up river to Dawson to check their salmon catch into the cannery. They had picked up the first catch of the spring run. We ate a quick lunch and reboarded our canoes, as the weather had improved slightly.

*Carl, hunkering down and waiting out a cold rain in the canyon
below Dawson. This narrow stretch of the Yukon often backs up ice
during the spring debacle, causing floods in Dawson.*

We paddled until 14:00 hours, when rain and fatigue caused
us to seek shelter on a small island near Fifteen Mile Creek. We
revitalized ourselves with hot Russian tea, then made camp. We
ate supper under our nylon fly. Ken retired to the warmth of the
tent. Neill landed face down in the mud going to the canoe for a
Sweet Marie, a Canadian candy bar that beats our Milky Way by
a mile. They became our favorite picker-upper when we first
found them in Moosehide, British Columbia. We retired early
and listened to the steady cadence of rain on the tents.

A quiet morning came. The downpour throughout the night
left small sesquipedalian puddles on the weather fly. Neill ran
the small beads of clear water off the edge of the fly and collected them in the coffeepot. The sun burned its way through a
cloud and streaked the sky. It promised to be an Olympian day.
Our question: would that promise be kept?

Following breakfast, we surveyed the storm damage. Our

equipment and canoes were wet. We had to dry out. Jim constructed a drying rack while I worked the ax. We needed dry wood for our fire. The center of downed spruce logs is dry, full of pitch, and good for that purpose. We gathered a large pile of chips and soon had a roaring fire. We spread our wet clothing and gear on the drying rack and wondered what this day would bring. We all had time to ponder the question, for we were together in our respective solitude. All things appeared to be at peace. The river, full and wide, slid by enroute to the Bering Sea. All was quiet with the exception of river sounds, the breeze, and a white crowned sparrow busily greeting the sunrise with his melodious patriotic song,

"Pure, sweet, Canada, Canada, Canada..."

By 11:45 things were dry enough to pack. We loaded the boats and paddled down river. Four hours and twenty-five miles later, we arrived at a small island. To our sorrow, the island was occupied. We moved on.

The river, for most of the distance, was lined with high granite cliffs. Within the hour, we found a spot near Forty Mile that had been a Canadian commercial company post manned by Jack McQueston. We had heard of McQueston the year before, having seen the name on the escutcheon of a car ferry working out of Arctic Red River on the Mackenzie River. The post was built to supply prospectors and miners digging gold from Forty Mile and Birch Creeks. A rival trading post was built by the North American Trading Company, and named Fort Cudahy. A Northwest Mounted Police detachment was sent to the region to keep order and build Fort Constantine next to Fort Cudahy. The fort was named for Charles C. Constantine, who commanded the detachment. Forty Mile had been the focus of gold mining activity near the Alaska-Yukon Territory boundary until the Klondike strike in 1896.

In 1896, George Carmack recorded his discovery of gold on Rabbit Creek, now Bonanza Creek at Forty Mile. It was also from this location that gold seekers came to search for gold along the many creeks in the Yukon basin. We looked forward to viewing the collection of cabins, which we understood to be in the process of restoration by the Canadian Government. The original cabins were abandoned after the discovery of gold on Rabbit Creek. Grubbing for gold at twelve dollars an ounce is all history. Will history repeat itself? We let the answer to that question simmer as we ate supper and then enjoyed a nightcap prior to bedtime.

On the 7th of July, we arose to a cold overcast day. I left the tent and started a large fire. We ate eggs, toast, and coffee, and packed out. The wind blew. A headwind, strong, canker-like, veering for reason or no reason at all, plagued us as we faced the elements. Three hours passed in the boats. We were cold and badly used. It was time for lunch, a fire, and time away from the wind. We enjoyed all three on a small space of bank in the shadow of the Ogilvie Mountains range. We noticed the valley was growing wider, and according to our map the razor-edged mountains reflected an elevation of 4,000 to 4,500 feet. Many of these mountains were capped with snow, dotting the scenery with a spectacular beauty.

We passed two bastions of rock, one on each side of the river named Old Man and Old Woman. They rose 150 feet above the water with vertical sides and spruce trees growing on their flat-surfaced tops. The river, half a mile wide and swift, kept them forever separated. Indian legend tells of a powerful shaman or medicine man who lived in this area of the river. Among his people were a poor man and his wife who were always arguing with each other. She was a nag. He was a poor provider. The last time he went hunting, he was gone from the village for many days, returning once again empty-handed. He and his wife started their constant nagging and bickering. Angered by her nagging, he gave her a kick that sent her across the river, where the Shaman changed her into a large rock as a reminder to all naggers. The Shaman then looked at the old man and turned him into a similar rock where he stood as a monument to laziness. There they stand forever separated, but forever in sight of each other, an admonishment to ungrateful people.

We left our cliff-side shelter at 13:45 hours, and fought our way to mid-river. We were determined to float – that is, sit low in the canoes and let the current work for us – thereby avoiding the use of paddles as much as possible. The idea worked for a short time as we enjoyed a respite from the headwind. Ken rested her back against the spreader behind her seat. I rested mine against the stern deck. We draped our legs over the gunwales.

Thirty river miles later, we found an island in the shadow of the Ogilvie Range. It was perfect for camping and getting a well-earned rest. The scenery was spectacular. As we sat around our campfire the wind died. The Tintana Valley was at peace. Ken drifted down the island and began to pick up stones. I watched until I could stand watching no longer. Quietly I walked to where she was at work and there to my surprise I found her forming the word Virginia with rocks on the sand. I called her attention to the fact that although her effort was a thing of beauty, her spelling could be improved. She had omitted the letter 'R' from her beloved state. Travelers before us had left their message written with the stones. The previous visitors had 'constructed' a large square room and written with stones *Living room*, to one side a pile of stones with *TV* and finally another 'room' marked *Bedroom*. We enjoyed the make belief rock home in the wilderness.

Sunday arrived with a slightly overcast sky. The winds of yesterday were still. By 06:00 hours, the camp stirred. Ken whipped up pancakes. The sun broke through the clouds. Things were just too beautiful to describe. The border, ten miles away, would soon be crossed. We all agreed that Eagle on Sunday was not in the cards. We needed a day without the canoes and this was it.

Our program, firmed up for the day, called for baths and gear check. We saw our duty and as Ken said, "exchanged one mud pack for another." The same happened to our laundry, but we were clean. I passed the afternoon reading Dick North's *Lost Patrol*. Ken started on *The Mad Trapper*. Neill became a civil engineer and tried stacking stones to control a small backwater pond on our island. The Yukon won. Jim slept. By late afternoon dark clouds appeared at the cardinal points. We hurried supper and hit the tents as the rain started. Sleep ended Sunday.

July 9th dawned bright and clear. We were up at 05:00 and had a breakfast that we ate slowly as we admired the beauty of the Ogilvie Mountains and the Tintana Valley. By 08:30 we were packed and off down north and east on the Yukon beneath a sky that held large patches of blue. We commented on the current and the twenty-one miles we estimated we had to paddle to reach Eagle, Alaska. We took fresh water from a small side stream located by *Castor*.

We left our small blackwater stream, thankful for its good fresh water, and felt the surge of speed send us on our way. We were once again in the grip of the main body of the Yukon River. By 10:30 we passed Boundary, Yukon Territory on our left hand, but could see little or nothing of the place where that small settlement once stood. Eagle lay eleven miles to the west and north of the abandoned town of Boundary.

We reached a thirty-foot cut through the trees that marks the boundary between the Yukon Territory and the State of Alaska. This boundary was established by survey in 1889, with William Ogilvie heading the survey team for Canada, and John Henry Turner representing the United States. There was supposed to be a brass marker on the left bank of the Yukon, but we did not stop to look for it. Our time changed from 09:15 to 08:15 as we crossed the imaginary line in the river. We were happy to be in Alaska, and thankful for the swift current that was pushing us along at about six miles an hour. We spotted fish camps along the banks, with their fish wheels tossing salmon into their large boxes. We passed Old Eagle, an Indian town, on our port hand. New Eagle, located in the shadow of Eagle Bluff, was dead ahead. We landed at 10:30 at the water gauge, where we moored our canoes. Jim was left in charge of the canoes. Ken, Neill, and I proceeded to the Post Office to pick up mail and find a telephone to call John and Lorna about meeting us at Circle in seven days.

CHAPTER V
Eagle, Alaska, Customs, and Northward

We walked to the U.S. Post Office, and found the Customs Office housed there also. John Borg, the American customs officer, greeted us. We told him we had just entered Alaska from the Yukon Territory. "How did you come?" he asked. "By canoe," we replied.

"Okay, give me your names and addresses." John tore off the corner of the local paper he had been reading, and proceeded to write down the given information. Then he crumpled it up and filed it in the wastebasket.

Formalities over, John asked what we needed. In helpful Alaska fashion, he drove us, in his ancient Hudson, to the only satellite telephone in the village. The phone was located in the dispensary in Old Town. We called John and Lorna, in Fairbanks, to have them meet us with supplies in Circle seven days hence. This arrangement worked to our advantage, since prices in Fairbanks were considerably cheaper than along the river.

Business over, we walked around Eagle, whose town limits were spread out along the banks of the Yukon. In 1905, Roald Amundsen walked to Eagle from the Arctic Sea to radio Norway he had conquered the Northwest Passage. A handsome stone monument, holding a bronze world proclaiming Amundsen's success in reaching the Pacific by sea from Norway, stood in front of the Post Office and Customs House.

Learning about the Eagle's Nest, Eagle's only restaurant, we thought a fresh salmon steak for lunch would be a real treat, also sitting in chairs and eating at a table. Sad to say it was not to be. A fire in the local powerhouse had closed it down. Our fresh salmon steak dinner would have to come another day.

We found Eagle buzzing with unhappy, young (20 - 35 years of age) Americans who had come to Alaska for 'freedom from government' to find President Carter putting some 56 million acres of land under the protection of the Antiquities Act. The woman running the hardware and grocery store was from California, her husband from Connecticut. We purchased sardines and crackers from them, then continued our stroll around town.

Signs were scattered around the town that read, *Antiquity is illegal, Park Service leave Alaska, Fight Tyranny,* and the classic *Crabgrass, lambsquarter and horsetails grow free, that's the way we want it in Alaska.* No one from the lower forties now living here was short on breath or words about Antiquities and the Bicentennial.

The town fathers had erected a small park-like area where cement restrooms were built for the tourists they expected to visit via the Taylor Highway. The tour included several other old houses, such as the warehouse near the river and the old Customs House, now a museum. It being closed, we looked through the windows and saw the Bicentennial certificate proclaiming Eagle a participant of that great celebration.

We sat on the steps of the museum to eat our lunch. A large yellow cat, whose friendly interest was not in us but in the sardines, soon joined us. He got to lick the can.

We left Eagle at 11:30 sharp. The water gauge station recorded 188 tons of silt per hour carried down the Yukon. We could hear it scouring against the hulls of our canoes. No one came to see us off. They wanted none of the tourist business.

The Yukon, strong, wide and muddy, accepted *Castor* and *Pollux* with firm pressure forcing us north and east into Alaska. On our port hand, a bad storm was brewing. Black clouds covered the sun, sky and our universe. Off Calico Bluff, a tremendous rock formation, thunder rolled like artillery. Beneath this bluff that looked like cotton print caused by the many minerals and varied rock strata, a boat of army recruits huddled waiting out the coming storm. With the second clap, a small moose calf darted from the black alders and plunged headlong down a steep bank into the swiftly flowing Yukon. The calf was followed quickly by his mama, who herded him, not without effort, out of the river and up the steep bank to safety. From all we could gather, the little guy wanted no part of combat, especially if the booming roll of thunder had anything to do with the exercise. He panicked and would have been carried off down the river if an older and wiser head had not been close by to save him. The young recruits looked like they wished their mothers were there to save them.

Lightning appeared in the storm, and we left the river for the safety of an island where we remained until the rain slackened, then set out again wet and cold. A short time later, we left our shelter and paddled to a small island near Seventy Mile Creek, where we made camp. A fire was lighted and Ken made hot tea. The storm was a thing of the past and all but forgotten. Supper, as always in the bush, was outstanding.

At 21:00 hours we began to fade. The feeling was strange and unreal until we remembered with a start that we had entered a new time zone when we crossed the border. It was one hour past bedtime, and it sure grew late and weary in a hurry as we said goodnight.

It was a short night, but my watch indicated it was 05:00, July 10th. I crawled from the tent to start the morning fire noting that the day was smiling. We drank coffee, admitting to ourselves that the sky had a few gray edges, but it was without wind. We ate breakfast, packed, and hit the river. It was a pleasure to paddle. We talked of the two empty canoes that John Borg had seen floating past Eagle the day before. Did some greenhorns lose their boats and/or their lives? Had they worn life preservers and drowned from the heavy silt filling the kapok and clothing so rapidly the items became cement blocks drowning the hapless wearers? Something the Indians had soon learned about life preservers and refused to wear them. Or did the canoers drown not knowing how to swim? Was it another mystery that would never be solved? The arctic and subarctic are full of such cases. A man disappears into the vast loneliness of that tremendous region and is never seen nor heard of again. We decided to accept the lost boat angle. We wondered if Don Witunik had such thoughts about our not returning.

Morning and river miles slipped past. We cleared Tatomduk River on our right, while the port hand view was of Windfall Mountain, Montauk Bluff, Nation River and a roaring basalt formation named Rock of Ages that has been fighting the Yukon River with a constant roar for countless eons. All were beautiful and interesting landmarks. In the afternoon, Kathul Mountain measured our progress as the sun closed its eye – or better yet, hid its face – and yes, it rained. I guess it was a combination of things such as the current, the rain, and the feeling of well being that caused us to think of making camp.

We located a small island after checking several that failed as campsites, and made a landing eight and a half hours – and fifty-two miles – from breakfast. We were once more on dry land and busy doing camp chores under a threatening sky. We ate supper under our weather fly, and watched as the clouds began to weep for reasons totally unknown to us, but probably not to God. Conversation dampened by the rain grew boring. We crawled away to our tents, happy to be cocooned from it all.

Just before sleep finally caught up with me, Ken was at the tent door watching the Yukon tear large chunks of earth from the far bank. The chunks made a great noise as they fell into the river. She turned and asked if I thought the two U.S. choppers we had seen hovering over the river during the afternoon had anything to do with the two drifting canoes at Eagle. I thought about her question but to the best of my knowledge, could not come up with an answer. Sleep won the hand. Pardon me Kenny...

The night of July 11th it rained hard. The inside of the tent sounded like hail on a tin roof. We were snug and dry as we lay on the ground mats listening to the rumble and roll of distant thunder in the mountains.

05:00 Ken was up and dressing. She dressed inside her sleeping bag where she kept her clothes so they would be warm to put on in the morning. We all slept in our long undies; at least we guessed Neill and Jim did too. It was still raining. I tried to talk her out of her madness but she left the tent for coffee. It was the first time I had been jilted by a coffee bean. At 06:00 the rain stopped and I crawled out of the tent to face the day. There was some gal outside yelling about blue sky and I had to see for myself. It was blue all right, but not so you could notice it. Tiny streaks of blue were just barely visible low in the east.

We ate a quick breakfast, packed beneath an angry sky, and by 09:00 we were on the river. During the morning, the sun made one feeble effort to shine but lost its battle to the ever-present clouds. The day grew darker. We slipped past Biedermien Bluff, 1,850 feet high, and on to Chester Bluff at 1,000 feet. Charley River appeared on our port hand and quickly bid us farewell. Then Bear Creek trickled into the Yukon and rapidly disappeared astern. By 12:15 Slaven Cabin appeared to port. We put in near the cabin and ate lunch. The sky grew darker. We thought of camp.

Following lunch, and under a burdened sky, we again faced the strong muddy current of the river and were met mid-stream by a heavy west wind. That did it. Wet OK, Rain OK, Headwind, rain, and no relief in sight – not OK. We made camp about two and a half miles west of Slavin's Cabin and settled for the day. The boats were pulled and our usual measuring stick carefully placed at the water line. We drank hot tea and congratulated ourselves on having beat the weather, or so we thought. Quiet came – the wind fell – the sun, by now a near stranger, put in a brief appearance. Then it rained like the seven capital sins. I guess no one ever beats the Alaskan weather.

During supper we talked of our short day. It had been fun regardless of weather and Ken's misfortune. She fell out of the boat at lunch and landed on the dry beach. Following lunch she jumped into the boat, sat down quickly, and missed the seat. It was a great performance, especially from the stern position in *Pollux*. Ken could not see nor appreciate my humor. We retired early to dry tents out of wind and weather, praying as we did for belle weather on the 'morrow.

At 04:55 things began to happen. First Ken moved, sat up and began to dress. Soon she was out of the tent and talking to the Coleman that was being difficult because of the soaking it had received during the night. Neill, next to greet the now never-ending day, was full of himself as ever. The ever ready, "Good Morning Ken," hardly died as Jim grunted his way back to consciousness. I listened knowing full well it was now my turn to rise. I just plain got up. The sky was clear and the all but forgotten sun was high in the east. The wind was still. It was a good day for canoe travel.

We ate breakfast and I cautiously asked if anyone had heard a noise in the night. Ken and Neill had heard something but did not investigate. The time – somewhere around 02:00. I heard something and crawled from the tent to investigate, but found nothing. Apparently the zipper on the tent flap had made sufficient noise to frighten the animal away from our camp. We let it go at that.

At 07:40 hours, we finished packing and shoved our canoes into the current. We passed a small island just west and twenty yards below our island, and standing in the willows sunning was our nocturnal visitor. A young moose cow watched our canoes through the willows, and we in turn wished her a good morning and a long life.

Our beautiful, clear, sunny morning wore on. We passed Woodchopper Roadhouse, abandoned, Webber Creek, Takoma Creek, where we took fresh water, and Takoma Bluff. We began to pass large swamp areas on both banks, a sure indication we were rapidly approaching the beginning of the famous Yukon Flats, a ten to forty mile wide, two hundred mile long swamp and marsh area that abounds in wild life and water fowl.

By 11:30 hours we had canoed twenty-eight miles. Since July 9th, we had covered 127 miles of the 145 miles between Eagle and Circle, Alaska, where we were scheduled to meet family on the 16th. We did not want to arrive at Circle early, and solved our problem by pitching camp. It was time for baths and laundry.

Ken served our usual hot Russian tea at 16:00. We drank it and gazed at the scenery many of our fellow countrymen will never see. We talked of game, Alaska, and where it all was destined to go, the Antiquities Act not withstanding.

A question was asked about moose, "Do they ever twin?" I answered, "Yes." At that moment my answer was proven correct. Not seventy-five yards away on the opposite bank stood a large cow and two very young calves. Slowly she walked her charges up the Yukon. It was obvious she wanted our island. We watched in silence until she disappeared in the alders to the east of us.

Chart work and notes commanded my time. I began to write when Neill called. I looked from the tent and spotted the cow standing near with her calves. Seeing us, she returned to the river and swam with the current to the far bank with the calves riding on her back. She had intended to night with us, away from wolves and in safety with her family. The same reason we used for choosing islands over the banks.

Ken cranked up the Coleman at 18:30 hours. Dinty Moore never tasted so good. Coffee followed supper, during which we discussed our plans and timetable. The problem as we saw it revolved around John and his flexibility, work-wise. He expected us in Circle July 16th. Thanks to the weather and the current, we could arrive on the 13th. Three nights in Circle with 1,200 miles remaining in our trip had little appeal, and yet we had to meet John and family. We decided that should the morning break clear, we would move on to Circle and camp there. Should the weather prove fickle, we would remain camped until the 14th, thereby giving us a day's rest, with a chance to inventory supplies. The idea of a day out of the boats had a certain appeal, and with that in mind we retired to our tents away from wind, bugs, and weather. The July days at latitude 65°, 30' North never end. The sun never quite sets. It bounces around for many hours, then slips below the horizon leaving a loom that appears to move from west to east before Old Sol peeks over the eastern horizon to begin again his travels across the arctic and subarctic sky. Another day was born for us at 05:00 hours. Our decision of yesterday relating to travel had to be faced. The morning weather, although not beautiful, was fair. I pocketed some small wood chips as we broke camp. Ken looked curious about it, but said nothing. We packed our gear, ate breakfast in silence, then agreed to move on toward Circle, twenty-one river miles away.

Paddling down the broad, majestic Yukon, quips were a way of passing the time of day and always made us laugh more than they were worth. Ken, stumbling over a rock getting to the canoe, asked me, "Using wood chips for chewing tobacco these days?" Neill to Ken, "Just washed your feet and can't do a thing with them!" produced another round of laughs. Ken to Neill who was scraping mud from his eyebrows: "Are you plucking your eyebrows, dear?" Wilderness humor, like freeze-dried rations, is only good in the wilds.

I remembered that our maps had shown the Yukon Flats as a wide meandering river with a multitude of channels and sloughs. As we moved toward our destination, the river became confused and difficult to navigate. The high cut banks prevented our seeing our destination, as we sat too low in the canoes for any type of view other than the river. I began tossing my wood chips sparingly at riverbank openings to watch where they floated. The main current would prevent them from floating too far down the sloughs before being pulled back into the faster current. Even so, we canoed a few yards down several before realizing our error. We had to stay in the main channel until we reached the slough on which Circle was located. The wrong sloughs could cause paddlers hours of work and sometimes days of travel time. We also passed many islands and bars, which added to the confusion. At long last we spotted Fourteen Mile Creek. It was time to locate the far left bank of the river, which we hugged until the village of Circle slowly came into view.

We landed at 11:45 hours, happy to have worked our way through the many islands and sloughs that mark the beginning of the Yukon Flats. The Flats are 200 miles long and ten to forty miles wide. We had canoed from an elevation of 2,060 feet at Lake Laberge to 596 feet at Circle. This translated into a two foot drop for every mile we canoed. No wonder we were doing wheelies around the bends.

Circle was built by Leroy Napoleon McQueston in 1893 at the top of the Yukon Flats, in an area as uninviting as its surroundings. In its early days, Circle was Interior Alaska's oldest major gold camp with a population in 1896 of 1,200 souls. The attraction of gold in the Klondike caused the town to die as people left the area to seek richer deposits two hundred miles up river. We were told that even its founder could not resist the gold fever, and he too left to seek his fortune in the more productive gold fields in the Yukon Territory. Today, Circle City's *Welcome* sign has the population at 68 citizens, the majority Indians. It is once more an area of attraction for adventurous Americans, who find their way to it as the most northern stop on connected U.S. highways.

We set up camp next to the area reserved for RVs, located close to the end of the Steese Highway, State #6, the last road from the north to the interior of Alaska. Circle is 154 miles from Fairbanks. Twenty miles out from Circle, the highway drops from 2,000 feet to 596 feet over gravel and washboard. We commandeered one of the three picnic tables from the camping area. Our camp on the bank of the Yukon faced east.

We met two RV loads of Detroiters camping along its high banks. The men had served in World War II and the women had been "Rosie the Riveters", helping to build planes and war ships for the boys up front. Retired, they had sold their homes and bought their RV's to travel and visit the fifty states.

After setting up camp, we went to the town's Trading Post, which was grocery store, post office, beer dispensary, cocktail lounge and café – named *Midnite Sun* – all under one roof. We called John and Lorna on the satellite telephone to let them know we had arrived safe and sound in Circle. John said they would leave Fairbanks by truck and make Circle at 17:00 hours, July 14th. Then we took advantage of under-one-roof Midnite Sun and cocktail lounge, and enjoyed the amenities of both.

Walking back to our tents, we came upon a worried army sergeant pacing along the bank and looking down river. He stopped to ask us if we had passed a boatload of soldiers up river. The boat of raw recruits we passed at Calico Bluffs had missed the turn into Circle, much to the chagrin of the Sergeant in charge. Apparently the two choppers failed to see them tucked under the bluff overhang.

"Yes," I said, then added, "Where did you get off putting those gravel crunchers on the river?" The Sergeant tried to ignore my remark.

Neill followed up with, "the river is for sailors, not a bunch of mud hens." The Sergeant was getting visibly disturbed and taking our joshing in poor humor until he realized Neill and I were old veterans like himself. We assured him it would be easy for recruits to miss the slough to Circle. He got them on his two-way radio and talked them back up river and into Circle at nine that night. After the sergeant put his charges to bed, we strolled to the Midnite Sun lounge for reminiscing about old wars.

On the morning of the 14th I awoke to a bright, hot sun and a beautiful day. It was 04:00. Jim was astir, the small Coleman was going, and coffee was close at hand. We had slept through another twilight night. The Arctic Circle is less than fifty miles to the north. We were indeed in the land of the midnight sun. Ken was soon up and hopping around the Coleman. Coffee was her business – don't meddle. We all got the message. Hot black coffee filled our cups, and we drank and watched the silent sun roll across the heavens. At 08:00, the restaurant opened. Ken was happy about that. We cleaned our cups in the river, and a little before 08:00 walked to the Midnite Sun Cafe, where we enjoyed a hearty breakfast. Rex, the post chef, officiated. Rex had learned his trade well as an army chef. Another veteran who had enjoyed the dismay of the raw recruits of the night before.

We spent the morning with Neill giving haircuts all around. A young Indian came by to watch the proceedings. Neill asked, "What do you do for excitement around here?"

"Go to Fairbanks," he answered hesitantly, and figuring that wasn't explanation enough added, "get girl, get clap, get home, get shots." After his series of shots, he then readied his traps for winter trapping, which made him enough money to repeat the "fun." Alice Carroll, his mother and town nurse for her clan, helped maintain the community's health and gave him his shots.

By mid-day, Neill and I adjourned to the restaurant. Ken joined us. We ate lunch, talked to Len and Gordon MacDonald, the owners, and waited the arrival of John and family with our supplies. At 14:00 Ken left to visit Indian town and locate the Carrolls. She needed to have her canoe shoes repaired and to talk to Alice about moccasins and other Indian artifacts she made and sold in the store. Albert, her husband, was the skipper of a small pusher he used to deliver oil and supplies to villages along the river. They were important citizens in Circle. Ken bought a postcard of the two of them holding up an unusually large King salmon. Ken said the Carroll home was clean and orderly. It was filled with family pictures, the main one being of her older son in Marine uniform and still serving his country.

Neill and I drank beer – a rather pleasant luxury, since we considered it unnecessary added weight in the boats. What better way to kill time, waiting for Ken to return from her town excursion?

The day remained clear, cloudless, and hot. We ran into a young man who had just arrived via the Steese Highway. He wanted to talk, so we listened.

"I'm Dan MacDonald from Eugene, Oregon, on vacation for

two weeks. I plan to raft the Yukon from here to Fort Yukon."
He was making the trip in a rubber survival raft, by himself.
He had never been in any sizable woods, much less wilderness.
But he was determined. We watched him depart twenty-four hours
prior to our leaving. He had sixty-five miles to float – alone.

At 17:00 hours John, Lorna, and Barb arrived with our supplies, the best of which was homemade wheat bread baked by
Lorna. Late afternoon, John and Jim unloaded *Castor* and paddled
to a small back slough to fish.

Ken strolled to the riverbank to talk to Michelle, who was
loading his homemade raft that was floated with empty oil drums.
He had a young Husky named Wendy. They were on their way to
Stevens Village, a commune of adventurers and artists. Michelle
was going to winter over with this group to paint and hopefully
make a name for himself. His trademark was his stovepipe hat
covered with army camouflage cloth. Ken called him "The Stovepipe Hatman." I read.

With no luck fishing, John and Jim returned and joined Neill
in the Cocktail lounge for a re-run of yesterday, and "to learn the
exact time of sunset" as reason for their late night behavior. Ken
and I ended our day around 22:00.

Sunday was the name of July 15th. I was up at 04:00 hours.
The day was beautiful, with mild weather, sun, and only a few
clouds. I guess I should have been happy, and yet I was sad. It
would be the last time to visit with John and his family. Ken was
soon up and the two of us sat at the very end of the Steese Highway. We gazed at the Flats, watching the shafts of early morning
sun paint the landscape of water and marsh grass in bas-relief.
We were waiting for the rest of our family to get up. When John,
Lorna and Barb arrived, we went to Midnite Sun Cafe for breakfast.

The wheels of time tortured and mauled the minutes away as
we slowly packed our gear. By 11:30 we were ready to bid each
other adieu – for we must walk our separate ways. Some must
remain while others, we in *Castor* and *Pollux*, count the miles to
the Bering Sea. With my thoughts unspoken, we paddled away.

The Flats – bug ridden, beautiful, wild, and lonely – were ours to enjoy. High water added to the river's confusion, making it difficult to read the water. We landed approximately twenty-seven miles below Circle. Thanks to John, we enjoyed happy hour and Yukon weather well laced with rain, which we accepted as a part of our river travel.

We made camp at Twenty Mile Creek. Three hours after our landing, we were joined by Dan. He was cold, scared and feverish with a bad cold. We were his safe world incarnate. We helped him pull his raft up the shingle to safety. We plied him with several drinks to help him ward off fear and loneliness and to fight his severe cold. Neill and I walked him to his tent. We did not expect to see him again along the river. His floating raft was much slower than our rate of progress.

The break of endless day came as a quiet morning with a few rain clouds, and a promise of a shy sun. By 04:00 I did the resuscitation bit and presented myself to an unimpressed world. The remains of last night's fire looked like it might burn, and I soon poked it back to life. By 04:55 Ken crawled from the tent and completed the scene. She soon made coffee, which we quietly drank as we communed with nature.

I checked the log. We were in our 25th camp, and this one too would soon dissolve as we worked our way through the hours and days, one by one, on our way down this wilderness river. Like prayer beads, these camps passed quickly through our hands.

By 08:15 we were packed and in the boats. The current ran fair and fast. Passing a small no name island, Ken spotted a sow black bear with a young cub on the bank. When the sow saw us she sent her cub up a tree and she took to the river. We swept past her on the strong current, Ken and Neill took pictures while Jim and I chatted about the bears.

We were in bear country. We knew we would meet others – black, brown, and possibly grizzly – somewhere along the river. From the experiences I have had with bear, I knew most stories were exaggerated. I also knew caution was the name of the game, that precaution against bear trouble is sound and wise, and chance of injury much lower. That is why I always insisted both boats carry firepower. For the purpose of self-protection, Neill carried the twelve gauge, loaded with alternate slugs and 00 buckshot, in *Castor*. *Pollux* had the .35 lever action carbine strapped under the comb where the bowman could easily engage it. I gave the .444 to John. In the years we have canoed the north country we have never had to fire a shot, but we have met bear, and had some nervous moments waiting for him to make up his mind whether to come toward us or stroll on up river.

The soundest advice is "do not feed the bear." A second solid rule is "keep a clean camp," and the third cardinal rule is "stay away from a sow with cubs." Nothing will cause trouble quicker than the startled squall of a cub. As a matter of fact, just trying to approach one of the little fellows is enough to get a person in real trouble. Cubs have caused more than one mauling.

During the time when most people canoe or hike, there are bound to be berries. These are a real temptation, and many a hiker or canoer has been run out the far side of the bushes when a bear decided to collect some berries for his meal. The Indians never go berry collecting without a scout with a gun to keep a sharp lookout for bear. Should you walk into a bear and are un-detected, move out of the area as quietly as possible. Always walk, if possible, with your back to the wind and make some noise. The Indians like to carry a can filled with small stones that they rattle. Some people insist on wearing small bells. However, I don't know how one keeps a bell from ringing when in the process of quietly moving out of a bear's way on a chance encounter. In my opinion, a can with a few small stones is much better.

Stay clear of a bear's food cache. If you are walking along a stream or near a thicket and detect a foul odor of decomposing meat stay clear. Old bruin likes to return to the scene, and is probably still in the area. Should you walk upon a kill that is partly covered with forest litter or branches, that is a certain sign a bear is nearby. The best method of handling such a situation is to leave the area as quickly and quietly as possible.

In the event you do run into a bear and old blackie stands on his hind legs, remember, stand still. If he woofs he might turn and run. If he runs you will have no cause for alarm. If, however, he stands his ground and begins to pop his teeth, that is your invitation to leave the area as quietly as possible. In doing so, always face the bear and move backwards quietly and slowly. Remember, if you run into bear there is a good chance he will leave, but I would not press my luck. If you are unlucky and have an encounter of the bear kind, as soon as you find yourself on the ground, lie still and don't move. Protect your vital areas by lying on your stomach and clasp your hands over your neck. By playing dead, you stand a chance of saving your life, but you can bet the experience will be painful.

Following the above lecture, I figured it was time to leave the boats for a quick stretch and lunch. We began to search for a suitable place to land, and finally located a safe place to attempt to leave the swift current of the river. We maneuvered our boats close to the shore, and expected our bowmen to make a bump and jump landing, which they did in expert manner. We grounded our canoes and watched as the Yukon boiled and rushed past on its course to the sea.

We ate a quick lunch and hurried back to the boats. Within the hour, we were scheduled to cross the Arctic Circle. The Arctic Circle is an imaginary line, but what hove into our view was all too real. Dan MacDonald was hung up on river trash and his rubber raft was sinking. As we approached him he yelled to us.

"I have a tire repair kit to patch the hole. I'll be all right," and waved us on. We kept going only to round the next bend in the river and find Michelle, Stovepipe Hatman, hung on a spit of land. His makeshift raft that he could neither steer nor propel was sinking. His big river sweep oars were too cumbersome to handle steering in fast water. His dog, Wendy, was only good for attracting bears.

"I've lost my maps," he yelled at us and added, "Ask anyone you might pass in a power boat to come pick me up." Of course, we assured him we would do just that, knowing full well that we would report both boys to the police in Fort Yukon.

At 14:30 we stopped for the day eleven miles north of the Circle. One half, or one hundred miles, of the Yukon Flats lay astern.

Camp #26 was pitched in the sun, which was hot. After setting up camp on our unnamed island, Ken and I went skinny dipping in a cold, silty Yukon. It was a quick dip ending with a warm sun bath on the sand. Neill and Jim bathed later.

Our last can of Pork and Beans brought to us by John was excellently prepared, *a la can*, by *Pollux*'s bowperson. It ended our Arctic day. Tired, we retired to the warmth of our tents, made warmer by the midnight sun continuing its rounds of the Arctic heavens.

Ken skinny-dipping in an ice hole on a hot Arctic day on Weir Island at Camp 39.

CHAPTER VI
The Arctic Circle and Westward

At 04:30 hours the camp began to stir. By 05:00 I left the tent with my notebook. Ken grunted as I fell over her on my way out. Jim and Neill were already up and had a fire in the making. Coffee would soon be ready and welcome.

There is nothing like sitting on a log above the Arctic Circle at 05:00 hours to record a personal history of four travelers on a common adventure through the Arctic. My spiral note binder was rapidly filling up with these details until the smell of hot coffee lured me from my chore to join the morning coffee club. We talked of our plans and what we hoped to accomplish once we reached Fort Yukon. We agreed we should talk to the authorities about the two young chaps we had met on the upper flats. Also, mail was high on our list of things to pick up.

Our immediate tasks this bright morning was to pack out early, reach the right bank above Toussaint Island, and ride the current to Fort Yukon, which is the largest Indian settlement in the arctic. At 08:15 we sailed, not according to plan, but as the Yukon directed. We left our camp via a back slough, and fought our way out of the current only to be presented with a sandbar and insufficient water for our boats. We turned left, solving our problem, and in time located Toussaint Slough. We fought again to escape swift water, only to land amid snags and deadheads that hissed at us and appeared to be speeding directly at us. We avoided disaster time and again until we were spewed forth on the right hand current, which literally shot our canoes into Yollata Slough and Fort Yukon

Normally, one would be pleased to see a small town, make a good landfall, and talk to people. This was not the case at Fort Yukon. We landed below a high cut bank amid dirt, debris, flotsam and mud. We walked to the general store through squalor and dust.

The fort was established as a Hudson Bay Company post by Alexander Murray in 1847. It was there that an unofficial boundary was declared between the Yukon Territory and the Alaska Territory, following Seward's purchase of Alaska from the Russians in 1867. The original fort fell into disrepair and was slowly torn down to provide firewood for the river steamers that plied the Yukon River.

First on our agenda was to go to the police post to check up on Dan and Michelle. If they do not make an appearance at Fort Yukon, a search will have to be made for them and our information as to their locations when we last spotted them would be invaluable. We talked to a very indifferent police Chief about our two up river friends. The Chief said they flew planes over the river everyday checking for people in trouble. We told him there had been none that we had seen since leaving Circle. Apparently, after thinking over our report, he became more polite. Driving by us as we were walking to the grocery store, he stopped and thanked us for our report. We tried. We hoped he would too.

We needed to purchase more supplies at the Fort Yukon grocery prior to departing for the last one hundred miles of islands and channels that make up the lower Flats. While we were shopping, the Southern Baptist Minister serving the community started a conversation with us. He recommended the Sourdough Hotel and Restaurant as a 'good' place to eat, so we went for a hamburger in the restaurant. It compared favorably with the poor restaurants in the south; the difference being, in the south we could choose another one. In Fort Yukon, this was all or nothing. The minister was a serious man dedicated to his profession. We enjoyed his company. We thought he had possibly been in the bush too long to judge gastronomic contests, especially since there was just one entry to judge.

Well, the company at the common table in the Sourdough Restaurant turned out to be interesting. Neill ran into a Florida acquaintance. She was visiting kin in Fairbanks, and had flown to Fort Yukon in a plane to do a bit of sightseeing. We got to talk again with the Minister. He was from Biloxi, Mississippi.

We were told that summer temperatures can reach 100°F, a point we were ready to accept following other days in the bright glare of the arctic sun. We had turned brown as berries – wintergreen berries. Back at the boats, we tried to talk Jim into a trip to the general store. No luck. He didn't need peanut butter this trip. We departed, thankful for mail from home, and thankful for the eager grasp of the swiftly flowing Yukon.

One and a half hours below Fort Yukon we made camp, happy to be again in the custody of Mother Nature. We were below the two mouths of the Porcupine River enjoying the peace and quiet of the wilderness when a violent storm broke, sending us to our tents early. We were glad to be dry and warm as we listened to the rain beat on the tents. So far on our canoe trip, we had managed to keep ourselves and our gear dry between the frequent summer storms that were hindering our progress.

During the night, the storm passed. A warm sun greeted us and helped dry our gear. It was 05:30 and a good time to start our day. Jim soon shot a hole in our egos by stating he had been up since 03:00. We ate a good breakfast. By 07:30 we were ready to depart when Ken saw a large black bear in the river. He was about mid-stream and making a crossing from the south to north, a distance of almost a half mile. We watched the old boy's progress in the swift water, where he swam with equal ease with or against the current. He reached our island and we departed.

The Flats are his, and we had no intention of debating the issue. We did not have an easy morning. Our course was west. We faced a gusty head wind that toyed with our bows, making canoeing difficult for the sternmen as they battled to hold against the relentless pressure of the wind. The river below Fort Yukon is wide with many channels and bars. She is swift, tricky, and mean to handle. For two and a half hours we fought the river and the elements. Finally, we agreed to seek shelter and wait for a break in the wind. The island we selected had a fine sand and gravel beach. It also had good water, fit for cooking and camp use. This water filled a 4- by 2- by 2-foot sand basin dug out by the river at flood stage during the spring debacle. Now, with the tip of the island exposed, the current hole became a catch basin providing clear, clean water, safe to use for personal consumption.

We played the waiting game with the weather for an hour, and ate an early lunch to help kill time. We made ready to depart when Neill noticed *Castor* had a leak that needed repairing. The boat had to be cleaned and dried before we could affect repairs, which required another hour's delay. I mixed epoxy and patched *Castor*. While we worked at our chore, Ken set to work washing clothes. In the hot Arctic sun and wind, clothes will dry in an hour. Neill checked the map and announced we had covered thirteen miles of river since breakfast. Reluctantly, we unpacked the other boat and pitched camp. It would have been a good day had the afternoon rain not arrived.

During the night the wind died and the world became still. At 04:45 I located my watch, noted the hour, and began to dress. Ken was soon up, and as she unzipped the tent an early lonely loon called from the marsh across the river. The call, mournful and clear, came to us announcing that the earth, at least our portion of it, was at peace. We ate breakfast in a quiet morning and turned to the canoes to inspect and check them for leaks. *Castor* passed the test. By 07:45 we were off, west and west by a little north down the Yukon, into a south wind that began to blow and threaten total destruction.

Three and a half hours later, on a bear trodden island full of scat, we abandoned the Yukon for shelter and lunch. The wind, that blessed west wind, tore at the river, shrieked at the sun hidden in a mantel of clouds, and kept us land bound. Our lunch stop became our night camp, and our west wind proved a spellbinder until the hour of three in the afternoon, at which time it died without requiem. The arctic sun and peace regained control of this semi-arid land. By that hour, our camp was set and Russian tea served as we sat and discussed the weather pattern we were experiencing. It occurred to us, if we were to reach our destination, we just might have to sleep during the morning and canoe in the late afternoon and evenings. We were morning people; late evening paddling did not appeal to us. We were on the river because we wanted to be there and we really had no timetable other than to be on our way home prior to the onset of cold weather. We concluded we had time and would resort to late afternoon and evening canoeing only if we had to.

During supper we watched a beautiful arctic evening unfold. The sun broke through the clouds, and as it moved west it painted the world with gold. I thought of the land we had traveled through so far on this trip. To me it was bleak, cold, hard, harsh, windy, and hot - an unrelenting, demanding land occupied by Indians and Eskimos, bear – black, brown and polar. It is the home of moose, Dall sheep, beaver, otter, mink, wolverine, wolf, fox, and fisher. It is the land of groaning fish wheels, gill nets, and raiding bear kills in the midnight sun. A land of mystique, mystery, and total enchantment. It is a wilderness that will allow travelers a peek at its splendor if they tread carefully and with respect for its quixotic ways. Our intent was to cross this land, east to west, by canoe. So far we had managed one third of our goal. As *Castor* and *Pollux* floated on the surface of a coffee colored Yukon, King, Red and Chinook salmon ran beneath our keels, and ran headlong into the fish wheels or gill nets of the Indians and commercial fishermen we passed.

This land and its history are as varied as its weather. It is a land of scalding sun at near midnight, or crying cold before the hour of arctic dawn. A land of 65°F below during winter, and a land both damned and blessed by all that experience it. It is much more. It is dangerous and not to be toyed with. It is Alaska.

As I drifted toward sleep, I resolved, if possible, to canoe other rivers in this majestic wilderness where life and death, violence and tranquility, storm and calm all hang by a thread. Where the friendship of the river people provides you with the information needed to survive their section of the river.

A ten o'clock high sun presented us with an east wind at 04:30 hours. We arose to find a river, not tormented as it was last night, but at peace. We had built our camp along a tremendous spruce that had fought the elements and lost. Like a gladiator, it lay on our island, stripped of top branches and all but a broken root system. Ken paced its broken length and found it to be one hundred and two feet. The diameter at the base was in excess of one yard. It had been a giant but found its match in the power and strength of the river that tossed it, perhaps during the spring debacle, high on our island like straw before the wind. We used it to anchor our camp on Deadman Island. Its supine position served as kitchen, breakfast nook and chairs.

Our camp on Deadman Island, where we set up our camp along a 102' spruce that served us as kitchen, breakfast nook, and chairs. We are canoeing through the flats.

Breakfast was over by 06:30. Our morning fire was dying. We began to pack. I expressed annoyance with our tents. Both were Jansports purchased for our Mackenzie trip a year earlier. Both now had broken fly screen zippers. Apparently, Nylon zippers will not hold up through two seasons of wilderness travel. The worst of our bug problems lay before us, and broken bug screens could become a serious problem.

Shortly after 07:00 I noticed a black bear near camp. I immediately finished what I was doing and returned to the group to tell them of my sighting. I also told them of the lone Indian who passed by at 01:00 in an outboard, bound for some place up river. I awakened enough to watch as he passed our camp. We all speculated on his possible mission, then continued to pack.

At 07:30 we watched as my friend of 01:00 hours approached from the direction of Fort Yukon fifty miles to the north. He landed his boat like the professional he was. As he walked in our direction, I walked toward him. He appeared to have a problem, and I was prepared to offer help if it was in my power to do so. His name was Artie Adams, from Beaver, Alaska. His greeting was formal and a question. Had I seen a fourteen foot jon boat within the past two days? "No," I replied, "Why?"

"Two young men, Willie Joseph and a fourteen year old boy, are missing. I found a jon boat floating down the river. I wasn't sure it was their boat. If it was, they had possibly drowned somewhere between Beaver and Fort Yukon." Artie remained stoical. We promised to watch for any sign of the jon boat and crew, saying we would stop at Beaver and let Artie know if we had spotted anything. As Artie departed, Ken yelled at him, "I saw bare feet tracks on our island."

Artie, misunderstanding the word "bare," yelled back, "Shoot him." With that he pushed his power boat into the current and departed. As the sound of his outboard motor died, we four stood in silence wondering about the fate of the two lost Indians. We checked our map. It was thirty miles to Beaver, and those miles were shot full of islands and sloughs that could easily swallow a fourteen foot boat and two men with little trouble.

We departed at 07:45. The slough was shallow and swift. Paddles were not the solution to the problem of getting our canoes to deep water. Finally, I jumped into the slough and lined the canoe to more favorable water. Thirty miles later we landed below Beaver.

Ken visited the local store, which also housed the Post Office. She met Elsie Pitka and ordered one pair of moose hide moccasins. She may see them by November. No money passed hands. Elsie told us Willie and the fourteen year old had floated into town two hours ahead of us. They had experienced engine trouble, but had made it home safely, thus bringing a happy ending to what we feared might have been tragic. The fourteen year old was Elsie's grandson. Artie met us at our canoes as we prepared to leave and confirmed the story. We parted in good cheer over the happy ending.

By late afternoon, we landed a mile below the town on a very dry, dusty sandbar, where we made our night camp in the wind and sunshine. I was awakened that morning at 03:30 by the sled dogs in Beaver. My first thought was that a bear had invaded the village dump. With that in mind I listened. The northern ravens were discussing the matter with little excitement. The world was safe as far as I was concerned, in that ravens never talk quietly when excited. I returned to sleep.

At 05:00 we all greeted a hazy day. The wind from the northeast was light, as was the cloud cover. The sun broke through the overcast in spots. We ate breakfast around Neill's fire, did our camp chores and packed out. We would soon be working our way down a very confused, slough-infested river.

By 13:15 we were searching for fresh drinking water, which we found in a gravel basin on the west side of Marten Island. These gravel basins are created during the spring debacle, when huge chunks of ice are grounded on the sand islands. The ice chunks are twisted and turned by the current, creating a conical shape cavity where the melted ice remains as water. The water does not stagnate because the water level of the pond stays the same as the river. The river water continually filters through the gravel, making clean, cool drinking water.

We walked through fresh bear and moose tracks where we beached our boats, determined to make a dry camp ahead of the rain. Our camp was set and supper in process when we decided to check our guns as insurance against a night intruder. A large bear had swum the Yukon from west to east, walked across our gravel bar and had crossed the back slough to the nearby alders while we were in the process of making camp. When we collected clear water for camp use we found fresh tracks that had not been there when we first inspected our clear pond forty minutes earlier. *It is reassuring to have first class fire power,* was my last thought before I said good night to Kenny and the world. Before sleep put me out of commission, I recalled Ken blessing the tent. The zipper that fastened the rain cover was now shot.

On the morning of July 22nd we were awakened by the call of a crane. We tried to locate her but appeared to be chasing a will-of-the-wisp. A stereophonic sound surrounded our camp, and in its midst a small golden plover was the only bird we saw working her way along the water line and attending to her morning chores. Everyone quit trying to find the crane, but me. I had to locate that bird. I got my field glasses out of the canoe and glassed the bar to the east directly into the sun. There they were, not one, but a pair of Sand Hill Cranes standing directly in the path made by the early sunrays. Everyone came running to take a look through the glasses. We watched the birds as we gulped our coffee. At 06:00 they departed on crane business and silence again reigned supreme. We walked to where they had been and found their ground nests. They were a mess of sticks and pebbles with no effort to hide or camouflage the nests or the one to two eggs in them. Some of the eggs had been broken and eaten by the gulls, some hatched out.

We ate breakfast, and while packing talked about the thirty mile run of yesterday. It had been an easy run with the wind behind us and the river fast, even while meandering around oxbows and bends.

07:00 we left camp. Peace Island passed to starboard as we

turned west into Horseshoe Bend. The water was slow today because we had the wind in our face – that is, from the west. A lone beaver smacked the water with his tail as we came near him. He dove quickly out of sight. The river flowed on and us with it. Large King Salmon rolled to the surface past us as they headed upstream to their spawning grounds. The stillness of the land was awesome. A second beaver surfaced near Ken, startling both of them. He hurriedly dove without sound in his haste to be out of danger.

At 10:30 we landed on a spit to stretch and take a break from the paddles. We lunched on King's Slough Island with a wide view of sloughs and marshes. As we approached Gull Island, we were greeted with raucous calls and side slipping gull-bombers warning us away from their nesting island. We hastened by, assuring them we meant no harm. It sounded like one gull kept saying, "shoo, shoo." Ken kept saying, "shoo, shoo," back at him. The gull got in the last 'shoo.' We increased our paddling to assure them we meant no harm as we passed by their community.

By early afternoon storm clouds began to gather in the southwest. The sky grew dark as we rounded Long Point. Down river from Windy Bend, we heard the ominous sound of an impending storm. We beached *Castor* and *Pollux* near the south end of Long Point and rigged our weather fly for rain. We were rigged facing northeast with a high sand bank and drift pile behind us. We pitched in this direction preparing for a southwest storm. The wind died, so we stood under our tarp and listened to the heavy rain pelt the nylon. The afternoon wore on slowly. Repeatedly, the question of continuing was answered by a check of the southwest weatherline. The sky continued to dump rain. By 16:00 we four jointly agreed to camp. We had to think of the cook. We ate supper around a large fire and listened to rain as we drank hot Russian tea under our weather fly. At 21:00 I said "good night," and crawled into the tent. We had traveled twenty-seven miles since breakfast, and sleep was no real problem.

07:25 hours saw our departure on a fast current. We negotiated "Now Cut Off." This was where the river had created an island by cutting off a tip of the Long Point ox bow. We noticed the river was getting wider and the cut banks steeper. We all knew our daily struggle had begun as wind, current, and sandbars fought to control the uncontrollable Yukon. We sat high in the seats and rode our two Old Town Otcas through it all. At 10:30, we landed to stretch our legs. By morning we had turned and twisted our way past Jackson Island on our right and Theodore Island on our left in a tortured river that jacknifed back on itself. We returned to the boats for an hour, then landed on Theodore Island to camp for the night.

July 23rd we were up at 04:00 hours, packed out by 06:00, happy to be swept away on a fast current. The sky gave us nothing to count on. 10:45 we landed on an island across from Stevens Village, the destination of our "Stovepipe Hatman" friend. The village was a commune of would-be artists, scammers, and other assorted types. We left, passed the Dall River, and stopped for lunch on a marshy spit approaching Chetlechak Island. We camped for the night on the northern tip of Chetlechak for a run of 27 miles for the day. The Little Dall River lay across from our campsite. We could see the slot that marked the end of the Yukon Flats

Ken, who worked in the bow of *Pollux* all morning amidst wind and slop, who cooked breakfast at 05:00, and who was up pushing the day at 04:00, looked to port and said, "Look at that beautiful sandbar." I looked.

The head wind blew strong and thunderheads peered at *Castor* and *Pollux* from beyond the rim of the Hamlin Hills. I called to Neill and suggested camp. He agreed and we landed on Ken's beautiful sandbar at Fort Hamlin. In a short time we set camp.

Our location looked more like home than did any of our many camps along the river. When the boats were unloaded and beached, we took advantage of the sun's brief appearance and bathed in the cold Yukon – one dry layer of mud for a clean wet one. Next came hot coffee and supper. Jim combed the area for firewood. He did a great job finding enough, considering our sand and alder patch had been underwater during the spring run off and all the good wood had been washed away. We reviewed our maps and discovered to our relief that tomorrow we would canoe a well-defined river for a change. The many islands and sloughs of the famous flats were behind us, at least through the next quadrant of maps.

On the 24th of July, I awakened at 03:50 hours and considered it respectable, although a little early. I lay still until 04:00. At that time the camp began to stir. Neill was up and using Jim's stash of wood to start a fire under a half buried spruce log. Ken blessed the Coleman, and soon hot coffee was served, followed by a good breakfast. We packed the canoes when the serious business of eating was finished. By 06:10 we were on the river.

The Yukon became narrow below Fort Hamlin. We had a definite current, although it did not run true. In spite of that problem we made miles. At 09:20 we slipped under the all steel bridge that supports service truck traffic and the Trans-Alaska pipeline. The bridge and line are to be admired for grace in engineering, but the area seen from the Yukon River is a veritable junk yard filled with old wrecked cars, pick-up trucks, and smashed oil drums – also known as Alaskan cactus. We continued on down river past the Big Salt River and on toward Sysie River.

Above Kalka Island, we passed an Indian fish camp on the far right bank. After much "hollowing" back and forth across the river with a fisherman, we understood him to say that Elman Pitka's camp was downstream. Elsie Pitka had given us a message to deliver to him. The current was too strong for us to make the far bank, so we continued on down river about one mile and located a good place to stop for lunch. We barely landed when Elman joined us in his riverboat. We gave Elsie's message to him.

She had recovered from pneumonia, you had a new grandchild and your daughter was coming later to join you. Elman was happy about the good news from his wife and thanked us for bringing the oral letter.

Elman's fish camp was about six miles below our location

on Crescent Island. He invited us to stop on our way, saying he had fresh white fish for us. We thanked him and he departed in his powerboat with his fifteen year old daughter and his ten year old grandson, who were helping him with his summer fishing.

We finished lunch and canoed the six miles to Crescent Island, where we located Elman's fish camp. The clean camp was up a high bank set in the poplars on Crescent Island. We admired his smokehouse. It contained 18" to 24" lengths of filleted salmon on the highest racks. The skin sides were cut in wedges and left on the skin, then hung by the tail, likewise the skeletons. Dog food hung on the lower poles in the smudge house and on poles on the outside of the house. The heads, backskins, and tails were also hung, but away from the smokehouse for the bears that might wander into camp and for the dogs. The Indians don't have to pay anything to fish, but have to register with the Game and Fish Commission, which controls the number of fish taken out of the river.

Elman gave us three good size white fish. He took them from a large plastic bag that he removed from a dug out permafrost hole covered with a large piece of spruce bark. This 1- by 1- by 3-foot hole was his refrigerator. The fish caught yesterday in a fish wheel were ice cold and firm. We did not stay long at the Pitka Fish Camp, although we were invited to spend the night if we so desired. We might have stayed, but Elman was in a hurry to visit Rampart City, thirty-five miles down river, for the purpose of talking to Elsie by satellite telephone. He was a small, wiry man, and needed help to transfer his large Johnson outboard motor from his work boat to a small faster one he used for quick trips on the river. Jim and I did the job for him. We then departed.

Locating a campsite can be a real pain at times. We checked many sites, but found none suitable due to steep banks covered with rocks. We fought our way another five miles down river before we were able to beach our boats for the night. We pitched camp on a slight grade, noting as we did that the spot was not the best, but it would have to do, in that we were tired of the river and sick of the wind that had plagued us throughout the day.

I cleaned our fish and Ken cooked the fillets for supper. We watched a large black bear move along the far bank of the Yukon searching for food. The bear was the second Ken had spotted since lunch. During supper we were blessed with guests. A cow moose with twin calves blundered into camp. Ken grabbed her camera and took pictures and our guests took to the river. Neill took the supper dishes to the river, cleaning them with sand, which he preferred over conventional methods. With the camp clean for the night and all leftovers thrown far out in the river to avoid attracting bear, we retired. Incidentally, the fish were excellent. I wish I could say the same for our tent sight. Ken talked me into setting our tent sideways on the hill rather than head to foot. Ken slept on the uphill side using me as a wedge to stop her slide down hill. I rolled against the tent side.

CHAPTER VII
Weather Bound and More Rapids

I greeted the 25th of July at 03:30, scrunched in my sleeping bag listening to the sound of light rain on the tent, and looked out the door at the day – a gray heavy day with wind and rain, cold rain. I returned to my bag thankful for the shelter provided by the tent, even though the zipper was now replaced by safety pins, the door was no longer watertight, and I kept sliding down hill.

06:00 Ken stirred and muttered something about hot coffee. About that time she became aware of the rain and hot coffee took second place on her list of priorities. She zipped her sleeping bag with a note of finality and returned to her slumbers.

At 07:00 the rain was still falling. The camp groaned and slowly greeted a wet day. Ken dressed and left for her daily fight with the Coleman. We soon joined Ken under our weather fly and had a fire going, which we took turns feeding, for we were determined to wait out the weather. More coffee? A great idea.

At 11:00, with rain still falling, Ken went to the tent to write letters home. She hoped to post them at Rampart, which was located some twenty miles down river. Neill and I got a different mile count from our present location to Rampart. Twenty miles, twenty-two miles, who cares? Our arrival depended on God, and only He could change the weather. We sat on our respective logs under our weather fly and waited.

The weather took many turns – none good. The sky grew dark; storm clouds were to the north, south, and west of camp. Rain came in sheets around the down river bend and raced across the mountainside to the south of our position.

We became engulfed in silence. A sad, silent sound like the sigh of a night wind began on Maypole Hill to the west. Jim, Neill, and I thought wind, but it was the calm before the storm. Rain fell at an ever increasing rate on the spruce, balsam, and poplar that covered the mountains across the Yukon from camp. A large black cloud peeped over the mountain across the river from us and spotted our position. All the clouds dumped their burden at once. We huddled under our nylon fly and watched the fury of the storm as sheets of water tore across the river and enveloped us. The rigging on our fly held. We were safe and reasonably dry as we watched the raging elements. The assault ended. Again a strange silence, an eerie stillness, until to the north, rain in great amounts began to fall. The mountain range faded, then disappeared. Rain raced down the Yukon like charging infantry and beat our frail shelter. Our lines held. We were safe. At this juncture, Jim threw up his hands and ran for the greater comfort of the tent. Ken, in our tent, was still writing letters home.

By 12:00, the storms of central Alaska abated. Neill and I left our safe havens to rescue our fire. The sky remained troubled and the wind flawed. Ken, forced from shelter by Mother Nature, disappeared briefly then joined us. We ate a quick lunch by a lively fire.

1:45 there was still no break in the weather. It appeared that "Ramp City" would have to wait until tomorrow. Neill and Jim took a gun and went in search of drinking water. Ken had the right approach to this fickle weather. She returned to letter writing. I sat with my notebook and wrote. The wind continued to flaw as the fire died. When Neill and Jim returned, we sat on a log and talked. It was a friend to friend chat that did nothing but fill in time and recall experiences we had shared on other rivers. As we talked, I watched the far bank for game. Spotting something, I called Ken for our binoculars and slipped to the tent to assist her in locating my find. At first I thought wolverine because of its small size. I concluded I was watching a bear. The glasses would soon clear up the mystery. It was a Black bear sow and two spring cubs.

The little cubs were not in a mood to mind, and went scampering down the bank dangerously near the fast flowing river. Mama's grunting brought one cub back, but the other kept going down hill half running, half rolling. All patience lost, Mama caught up to him, and with a wop across the chops, had him scampering back up hill into the safety of the conifers. She lumbered up behind them. This was certainly bear country. Neill, Ken, and I recalled seeing eight bears in the past two days: seven blacks and one big brown.

All through the night of July 26th the wind moaned and sobbed around our camp and screeched in the adjacent mountains. Rain fell, then ceased. Silence, the hard yet malleable kind, ended with rolling thunder. At 04:00 I crawled from the tent and assessed the coming day. Gray, overcast, windy, nubs cover; all in all, rotten. I gave up and returned to the warmth of my sleeping bag. Ken slept.

At 06:00 Ken dressed and left the tent to prepare breakfast. She left the tent fly open and I viewed the heavens. What a mess. I dressed and joined Neill and Jim in setting the morning fire. We drank hot, black coffee.

07:30 we started breaking camp, destination: Rampart, population 40. We left our east bank campsite above Hess Creek at 09:10. Storms danced around Maypole Hill. The wind, fickle to the end, saw us depart with a shove then jumped into our faces. By 10:30, Point No Point lay on our port hand. Jim spotted a black bear. We did our best to photograph it, but lost. We also saw a mink, again no pictures. He was too fast for us.

We passed many fish wheels and marveled at their capability. These primitive perpetual motion machines turn endlessly, hour by hour, throwing salmon into their maws. The government controlled the number of salmon caught by these wheels. After a predetermined count, they stopped the wheels on the lower river so that people living farther up river would have an opportunity to fill their wheels.

One of the many fish wheels that are used to scoop up the salmon on their run to their spawning grounds up the tributary rivers flowing into the Yukon.

Chicago Lakes, really a large swamp, lay behind Point No Point. Long miles later, we saw the last of the elusive Point problems. We passed Minook Island as our immediate destination, Ramp City, lay before us. Clearing the last point, Ken spotted a large black object in the water. It was a dead black bear, ample evidence of the constant war between man and nature for survival. As we passed Ken's find, the fish wheels continued their endless groaning and turning, unmindful that the fish they scooped from the river undoubtedly caused the demise of old blackie.

We landed at Rampart directly behind the post office in Ramp City. A small seaplane lay to the west of our position. It belonged to the one man who controlled the commerce and civic order in the town. We shopped in his store. A fifth of Seagram's 7 Crown cost $11.50, $1.60 for a loaf of white bread, $2.65 for one dozen eggs, and $6.00 for one pound of hamburger. We paid our bill and left to find a campsite.

Six miles later, we camped on the northeast end of Six Mile Island. We were once again in the wilderness of central Alaska, and once again at peace. During supper, we enjoyed hot drinks and talked of the coming rapids we would face on the morrow.

Our night of July 27th passed, but the storm did not. Wind slapped at the tents and caused the broken rain fly to pop and luff. At 03:50 I crawled from the tent and looked at a cold leaden sky of Alaska's endless summer day. Futile. I crawled back into the tent and my sleeping bag. I thought of the coming rapids. Such places, in nice weather, can be a challenge. In a headwind, a man is foolish to attempt such an endeavor on a wilderness trip, where there is no help around the next bend and survival depends on one's ability to keep food, gear, and self dry.

05:30 Ken woke up. I heard her leave the tent. A light rain began to fall. As it struck the tent, I dressed and collected my pocket litter. It is interesting to watch how values change. A compass goes without saying. The hunting knife becomes more important than a wallet or glasses. Rifle shells are guarded as one guards money. Fish hooks are all important, and a finger nail file has no real value at all, I thought.

Well, I'll play the game with the others. I joined Ken and Neill by the fire and asked, "What do you two keep in your pockets?"

They looked askance; the game needed further explanation. "That is to say, what do you consider of great enough importance to wilderness survival to keep in your pockets?" They started digging.

Neill held out a compass, pen, comb, tweezers, two 12 gauge shotgun slugs, and a Swiss army knife with a small finger nail file attached. Ken showed a red farmer's bandana, three .35 rounds, a compass, and a small purse fingernail file, which doubled for a pick to work on the tent zippers. Jim, in the outback collecting firewood, didn't join the game. I bowed to the obvious. Fingernail files also have other uses in the wilderness. Nothing should be discounted as unnecessary when that is all that is left to use.

06:30 Jim took a gun and set out to explore our island. He looked for and found fresh water. Light rain continued to fall, and the west wind played with the tents. Ken started breakfast. Pancakes! What a way to start our 41st day on the Yukon. We ate by the fire and speculated: would the weather let us move, or not?

After breakfast we arranged our gear under the weather fly and stood in its shelter out of the rain. One by one, we returned to the tents, thus marking up another day of no movement on our travel record. I slept. Ken read the *Lost Patrol*, by Dick North.

Early afternoon, Ken left to reassess the day. It was still rotten. We passed the afternoon reading, sleeping, and standing around the fire. 17:00 hours, we indulged in our nearly twelve dollar bottle of Seagram's, then ate supper.

On the 28th of July, a new light appeared in the east around the usual hour of dawn in this land of almost never ending day. The inside of the tent was like a large blue dome. I knew the sun was smiling and the gray clouds were skulking over the horizon. A quick breakfast and fast pack out put us on the river making good time by 07:00.

We passed Twelve Mile Island, saw a black bear along the bank, paused at the paddles, and floated with the current to watch the bear search the water's edge for salmon. He wasn't having much luck so we moved on, leaving him to his morning hunt.

At Garnet Island we stretched and talked about Garnet Creek, which we knew to be on our port hand. We needed to refill our jugs and water skins. The Yukon is potable but silty, with a type of silt that never seems to settle to the bottom of water containers no matter how long the water is allowed to stand. Yukon water in this section of the river could be used as a last resort, but we preferred cold spring or creek water. We cleared the west end of Garnet Island and fought to cross the river to get to the confluence of Garnet Creek and the Yukon. What a beautiful sight: clear water and fish. We saw salmon, grayling, white fish, and suckers, all resting on the gravel bottom undisturbed by our presence. Bear had been fishing, for there were bear tracks and scat on the bar and along the creek. We fished this creek, which was one of the most beautiful we had seen so far on our trip. Jim and I caught eight grayling, which we cleaned. We filled our buckets with creek water to keep our filleted fish fresh until suppertime. We stowed the buckets under the stern seats. We filled our water containers and reluctantly left this haven for the roiling waters of the Yukon.

Lunch at 13:15 was quick. We ate on a large flat rock on the south bank of the Yukon. We had the Yukon Rapids near Raven Ridge on our minds. Rapids can never be taken lightly when one has to face them, and are not soon forgotten once astern.

Following lunch, the tempo of the river changed. We first experienced roils and cross currents, which wrinkled the surface of the river and caused an odd feeling in the canoes. As the roils increased so did our speed, and we knew we were making miles. Near Raven Ridge, we spotted a fish wheel and talked to the owner, who was at the wheel cutting salmon. We asked him about the coming rapids. "Stay left," he yelled.

He was an old hand on the Yukon, and realized the danger of rapids, especially to canoes. Staying left as we approached the rapids would avoid some of the heavier water. Our answer probably never reached his ears due to the wind and river sounds, but we yelled our "Thanks" just the same.

In Ramp City, someone had said to stay right. I wasn't happy with the answer as our maps showed more danger, so I was glad to see this fisherman tending his wheel at such an opportune time. It had become apparent that a well-stationed person was always present when we needed advice about the river. We knew the Yukoners were aware of our travels, and we had wondered how much help they were giving us without letting us know. The wilderness people were like that. They depended on us to pass their messages to their families. They surely must be looking after us. I remembered Don's goodbye, "see you someplace." It had a double meaning for the Yukoners, which we were soon to find out.

A short way down stream, we rounded a bend and found ourselves surrounded by beautiful mountains. We were also greeted by the never to be forgotten sound of fast deadly water. The hiss, roar and deafening thunder of such brute power makes a lasting impression, especially when you are in an eighty-five pound canoe that would not last two minutes in such water if not properly handled. Nor, for that matter, would the occupants of such a vessel.

We were fast approaching the rapids as we shot through roils and current pressure lines, ever mindful of the tormented water that thundered on our right hand. Facing the challenge, we popped through several haystacks, broke the current line and breathed a sigh of relief as we sat listening to the sound of doom fade astern. Both boats worked the current well.

When all was a thing of the past, I recalled watching my bowman as she sat, firm as a rock, not three feet from destruction bobbing and pitching through those haystacks. She had spent time on other rivers with me, always trusting that I would do the correct thing in tight situations. Somehow I always have. I guess that is the first real test of teamwork, in that without her in the bow serving as eyes for our canoe, I am certain I could not manage to guide us in safety through the rough spots we have faced together.

Six miles below the rapids we located a good campsite, where we soon settled with the boats high and dry and the rapids a thing to talk about for the rest of our lives. We ate our fish caught in Garnet Creek, and at 21:30 bid a four o'clock high sun good night.

At 05:00, I was conscious of two things. It was Sunday, and it was July 29th. I crawled from the tent and found a quiet morning and sun. The night dew lay heavy on the grass and great beads of dew and condensation hung on the tents, reflecting the sunlight like drops of silver. The Yukon in all its splendor flowed quietly past camp, the roar and violence of yesterday now a memory. One match and a little effort produced a fine fire. Ken collected wood. We drank coffee strong, black, and hot. The smell of Good Old Java brought Neill and Jim to the world of the living.

Sitting on a log and three cups of coffee later, we speculated on the day. Since the sun continued to shine, we washed out the canoes, sorted and repacked gear while Ken ran the food inventory. By 09:45 we were on the river. Noontime we put our paddles aside and drifted with the current as we watched a young fellow work a long gill net.

Watching him take several salmon from his net reminded me we had not yet had our planned salmon steak dinner. Unfortunately, he was too far across the current for us to reach him. The speed of the current would carry us far below him before we could paddle to the other side of the river.

Now fortune turned in our favor. Having finished pulling that net, he got in his outboard and crossed the Yukon upstream from our canoes then swung down the east bank to check a second net. This time I knew we were in hailing distance. "Would you sell us one of your salmon?" They were still flopping in his boat. *How much fresher can you get?* I thought, smiling to myself at the prospect of fresh fish for dinner. "It's yours for the asking!" he yelled back.

We still had a bad current to cross, but a worthy goal puts more muscle in the effort. We landed smartly on the shingle. He was Bill Fliris from Colorado. His wife was Maria, who hailed from Oregon. Ken took pictures of us as we stood around talking. They had been homesteading along the Tozitna River for five years. They fished commercially in the summer, and trapped for a living throughout the long winter. They reminded me of John and Lorna – two more pioneers enjoying the good life of Alaska. Bill picked up the humpback that was still flopping and hung it on his scales. It weighed 34 pounds. "Take this one," he and Maria both insisted. They would not let us pay them for it. Our thanks seemed inadequate for such a gift. But like Ken said, "Mother always said one should learn to be as gracious in receiving as in giving." We were keeping them from their business and ourselves from getting on down river to catch up with Neill and Jim. We waved goodbye and pushed off.

Neill and Jim had beached *Castor* less then a mile down stream on a shingled bank. They had picked a nice place for lunch. They oohed and ahhed over the size of our fish, which I cleaned on a flat boulder that we had first used as a lunch table. Both of Ken's hands held together were not big enough to hold the roe. We carefully laid it in a pan of water with the steaks, ready for the evening meal.

We departed for Twelve Mile Island and landed at 15:00 hours, pitched our tents, bathed in an ice hole pool on the tip of the island, did our laundry, and sat down to hot tea. We looked forward to a salmon supper, and best of all, supper in the sunshine. The sun held warm, and Ken produced the impossible by actually cooking not only the salmon but also the roe on our camp stove. Fish and roe were a gourmet treat after all our freeze-dried rations.

We were awake before the hour of 05:00. I poked up the fire. The morning of July 30th was bright and cold. We agreed not to rush the morning. We lingered over coffee, ate breakfast and departed at 07:40. We moved down the south side of Twelve Mile Island searching for drinking water. We crossed to the north bank, where Neill and Jim found Jackson Creek: glacial water, clear, cold, and sweet. We filled our skins and laid them on top our weather covers, which we had been keeping on the canoes since Five Finger Rapids. We continued toward Tanana Island and Mission Hill. The river grew wider, but was calm with a strong current.

CHAPTER VIII
Tanana and Death on the Yukon

09:45 we landed at Tanana Village, where we shopped at the Alaska Commercial Company. The managers were friendly and helpful. The prices, by lower forty-eight standards, were high. We bought Washington State apples for fifty cents each. The proprietress told us a sixteen year old Indian boy had drowned on the 25th, prior to our arrival. The Alaska State Police were organizing a search for the body, and were in the village waiting for divers from Fairbanks to come search the river.

Tanana is located on the north bank of the Yukon and Tanana River, and directly across a wide fast stretch of river from Long Island. The current, heavily laden with silt, is reported between eight and ten miles an hour. Chances of locating the body were not good.

I finished my shopping and returned to the landing, where Neill was watching the boats and talking to Hugh Harrison, one of the troopers stationed in Galena. Harrison said he was born in Florida but had come to Alaska several years ago. He was in Tanana because of the drowned boy.

Hugh said, "We have ten or twelve teenage boys drown a year in my district between Galena and Tanana, primarily from too much drinking. The boy's Granddad is camped below the village on the right bank waiting for his return."

"You don't expect to find him alive do you?" Neill asked.

"No, but his Granddad will remain there until the body is recovered or the search is ended," Hugh answered. Neill changed the subject to business. "How is the Alaska Commercial Company impacting the native Alaskans?" Neill asked.

"The company pays the workers, pays the fishermen for their salmon, processes the fish, and resells the finished product to Alaskans and to the Lower Forties. It is an attempt to change Alaska from a barter system to a monetary system," Hugh explained.

Ken returned from the store. It was time for us to depart.

"Keep a look out for a body along the river," Hugh said as we boarded our canoes. "We'll look you up in Galena, Hugh," I answered.

It was good to be on fast water again, mindful of wind, weather and current problems. It was good to be away from the sad village, where each of us had added a donation toward the purchase of gasoline for the search boat.

All that was left behind us, or so we thought, until we rounded a point and saw the old man alone under a makeshift shelter. He was curled up like a dog on one air mattress, with a second fully spread, waiting for a grandson who would never come home. The loss of a relative or near friend is a terrible event for us all. The Yukoners never say goodbye. They say, "we'll see you someplace." In this harsh land, along this long river, no one can say with certainty where "Someplace" will be. Don Witunik's farewell took on a deeper meaning.

We paddled close to the shore for several hours in the vain hope that we might find the boy's body. Past Steamboat Slough and Tozitna Island, we began to search for a good spot to camp. Steamboat and Tozitna supplied too many bugs and/or too much mud. Circle Island was selected as the best we could find, and we pulled our boats, happy to once again enjoy the beauty, harmony, and tranquility of the wilderness.

In the west-southwest, dark clouds were gathering – a summer storm was in the making. We drank hot Russian tea and I thought of the old Indian on his air mattress, alone in his grief and sorrow, beside a mighty river that had been his highway, source of food, and livelihood. A river he undoubtedly knew and trusted throughout the years had claimed his grandson. What must he think of the Great Spirit that controls us all? What now, in his sorrow, in the face of a gathering storm? I set my pad and pen aside but the question of the old man would not leave me. The storm that gathered in the southwest passed to the north of us. Ken had supper ready.

July 31st began at 04:10. Jim was up and had started the fire. Neill soon joined him. Ken joined the living at 04:30 and tried to light the Coleman. It was out of gas. As last dog, I received a meager welcome from the group and filled the Coleman with gas.

We started down the river at 07:25, and at 08:15 were off Basco Island. We met a pusher, *Romona II*, with a load of fuel oil for Tanana. The *Romona* saluted us with a short whistle and we yelled back. This sight made us aware we were slowly working our way through summer and that winter was a few short weeks away. We knew we had many miles yet to cover, so we dug away with our paddles and hurried the canoes westward.

At 10:15 we paused on Little Joker Island to stretch our legs. We checked our maps and found we were covering six plus miles an hour over the ground. Thirty minutes on the bar, and we were again on the river. Off Swanson Island we met our old friend "head wind." We pushed on. The river chop soon turned to slop, with a fast and tricky current making life one real tough problem manning the bows of *Castor* and *Pollux*.

We cleared Painter Point at 12:00, and thirty minutes later grounded the boats on a gravel bar north of Clay Island. It was time for a well earned lunch. Shortly after 13:00 we pushed off. We warily eyed the storm clouds on all sides of us, and listened to the deep voiced volley of thunder roll across the heavens. We were again in the grip of a gathering storm. With minutes left on the dry side of the coming maelstrom, we hurried on.

West of Clay Island slough, we spotted Weir Island. The question was, could we make the island and pitch camp ahead of the storm? We made Weir Island, but lost to a quick heavy shower. Following the rain, we set up camp then all took showers, if you can call a bucket of silty water heated over a fire a shower. We felt clean as we huddled around the fire and watched the arctic sky toss gray and white clouds like snowballs at the struggling sun. Finally the sun won, putting in an appearance in all its glory. What an afternoon to loaf at our 39th camp. Ruby could wait.

Supper was served at 18:00. Freeze-dried Chicken a la King, Bisquick biscuits baked in an iron stew pot used as an oven over the open fire, and tropic butter tasted great. We watched as the sun tipped low on the western rim of our world, and we listened as hordes of gnats gathered for an evening assault on our persons. This gnat activity became very personal and unwelcome at our toiletries. They finally drove us to the shelter of our tents and ended our day on this beautiful and grand river.

Night passed quickly, and the morning of August 1st started at 05:00 hours. We ate a quick breakfast, and at a quarter to seven a low straight line of clouds hung above the river to the north and below the mountain peaks.

I commented to Jim, "Weather." He looked at me and grinned. The sun was out, and only a scattering of clouds was visible elsewhere in the sky. "We'll have a head wind today," I told Jim, "Count on it."

We passed Liner Island at 08:45 and swung west down the north bank of the Yukon. Around 09:00, small cat paws appeared ahead of our canoes and toyed with the current roils. This was the prelude to a surging west wind that produced headwind and a good chop. We struggled westward. Neill and Jim heard the sound of fresh water, which we needed for camping. They shot *Castor* into the current ahead of a large poplar tree hung on a bar by its roots. I was too late to follow them. A strong current caught *Pollux* and I maneuvered around the bar. I called to Neill and told him we would pick up fresh water at the mouth of the next side stream. With that message, we left Neill and Jim in the mouth of Montana Creek.

One and a half miles later, Ken and I found Sunshine Creek, entered and added to our fresh water supply. We sat in *Pollux* in the cold water of Sunshine Creek. Ken filled our jug and water skin. I fished. No luck. Within thirty minutes, Neill and Jim joined us and we promptly departed Sunshine, heading toward Nine Mile Point with *Castor* leading the way into the increasing chop of the river. This leg of our trip took another one and a half hours. Ken took a reading of the west wind with her Wind Meter. It continued in gusts of seven to ten miles per hour, making paddling tough and creating a real slop problem for the bowmen.

At 11:00, we rounded Nine Mile Point well astern of *Castor*. We had been unable to hail Neill, probably due to wind, and had landed to stretch and take care of personal chores the gnats like. When Neill realized we were not in view astern of *Castor*, he stopped paddling and was drifting, waiting for our arrival off Nine Mile Bar. We clawed into the wind and finally hailed him through a wind, chop, and cross current slop that made a real mess out of the surface of the river. We pulled along side and agreed it was time to eat, and if necessary beach the boats.

Lady Island looked like a good spot, so we headed banging and splashing our way toward her headland. The wind tore great chunks out of the Yukon and hurled them over the bows and sides of *Pollux* and *Castor*, only to have them slide across the splash covers and return to a very angry river. We made the headland at 11:30 to find that the Lady had mud, rocks, and few flat spots for camping. She did offer firewood, so we started a fire. Jim was very wet and cold. We hugged our fire and ate cold beans, bread, pickles, peanut butter, and drank from our water skins while the wind blew with fury from the west.

The afternoon was spent feeding our fire, sleeping on the gravel, and waiting for a weather change. It did not come. At 16:00 we pitched a camp of sorts, and Ken made hot Russian tea to warm us and give us energy. She then hit the tent to write. Supper, I was certain, would be the only cheerful spot left in an otherwise dull, damp, wind whipped day. As I sat on a log to write my notes, the sun peeked from behind a cloud, then not liking what it saw, quickly disappeared. Dark, ominous clouds gathered to the west and north of camp. Will the weather break by morning? That was rapidly becoming our eternal question.

At 03:00 hours I crawled from the tent and looked at a heavy gray sky. There was little light except in the east, where the first red, pink, and blue of a far northern dawn was visible. Other than that small token of hope, the subarctic night smelled of rain and spelled storm. I returned to the tent. The prospect of a full day on Lady Island was grim. Mud, bugs, wolf, bear, and moose tracks, plus the steady hum of the ever present mosquitoes and the thud and slop of a storm tossed Yukon River did nothing for my disposition. Being storm bound always runs counter to my nature, so I returned to a restless, fitful sleep.

At 05:30 the day, overcast and leaden, was quiet. Jim snored on in his tent, unmindful of the prospect of a promised incarceration on Lady Island. Neill, Ken and I gathered by the fire to smoke mosquitoes. We agreed we would attempt to escape Lady Island if at all possible. Jim crawled from his tent and we set to packing. By 07:55, we were on the river, happy to be moving in spite of the promise of a storm. At Lady Point we took on fresh drinking water from a small stream that dumped ice water into the badly swollen Yukon.

We came to Chokoyik Island, and midway down the north side of Chokoyik the wind began to blow, driving us to the north shore in an effort to find some kind of lea. Henry Island lay astern. We took a break from the paddles to let the wind quiet down, then rode the current to Moose Point, where we ate a light lunch.

Camp on Mouse Point. We were watching a rainstorm on Kokrines Hills (VABM 3,669')

Following lunch, we swung west into Western Channel. A stiff west wind made us lose interest in making miles. We agreed to camp. We checked Oyle Island with no luck, than paddled between Florence and Edith Islands – both mud and alder mosquito traps. The Yukon was high. The maps showed more islands in the river than we were finding dry and habitable. We passed Florence Island with its high cut banks. Mid-channel our chart showed a small island with a head gravel bar. We arrived at the spot only to find the bar and our island under twelve to eighteen inches of water. No camping there. In due course, we arrived at Mouse Point, which at one time had been a part of Mickey Island until the river cut the point off. Here at last was a dry bar. We landed, pulled our boats, and established Camp #41.

On the morning of August 3rd, I awoke to the sound of heavy horsepower on the river. Looking out the tent flap, I saw a large pusher passing our camp. It was the same vessel we had seen as we departed Tanana several days earlier. I wondered about its cargo and destination, then returned to sleep. 05:30 I awakened in time to see Ken leave the tent. She had to have hot coffee in the morning or else. I dressed and followed her to the still smoking fire of yesterday. We left Mouse Point but not before we spotted a cow moose and young calf swimming in Victor Slough. The contrast of a thundering pusher and a concerned cow and calf swimming in the river made the Alaskan scenery complete. Neill had seen a wolverine across the slough from the camp the previous evening. It all added to our pleasure and excitement.

07:05 we departed Mouse Point west bound. We passed the tip of Mickey's Island, named Lone Tree Point, on an easy current. The river was broad and quiet. We estimated the distance from bank to bank at three miles. Working the boats with the current, we slid by Emerald Island on our port hand and Hard Luck Island broad on our starboard beam. The day was perfect. As we swung full west, Kokrines popped into view with its Spirit Houses cemetery.

Spirit Houses are the tombstones, so to speak, for the graves. The departed Indian's belongings, such as knives, bows, arrows, and clothes are kept in them. The storage of such items is kept sacred and used only in the event of need for survival by the living. Kokrines appeared abandoned. We did not stop. Horner Hot Springs could not be seen, although we made an effort to locate it as we neared Fox Island. Ham Island lay to port, and Dasha Island slipped by to starboard as the Kokrines Hills monitored our progress. We were making good miles this beautiful day, and we knew it.

On Nine Mile Island we paused for lunch, then hurried on toward Ruby. We passed Straight Island on our right and the Melozitna River, but did not stop. Ruby had supplies and our mail from home. We wanted both, and Ruby was in sight.

We landed at 13:30 just below the eight-by-eight log Post Office at the bottom of the slope where the town started. Ruby's homes were set in blocks up a steep hillside and marked off by well oiled streets. The houses had electric ringer washing machines sitting on the porches. Everywhere, government health services were in evidence. One old soul was sitting in the open door of her house in a wheelchair with her legs wrapped, the left one set out straight on the raised chair leg. It would have been impossible for her to wheel it or have it wheeled along the streets. For a blind man, the town had built a wooden hand rail and walk from his house to his outhouse. The old folks and the very young played along the riverbank. One old gentleman vigorously shook Ken's hand and yelled to all of us, "Welcome to Ruby."

The Ruby Post Office, where we picked up mail from home. Ruby was built up the hillside to the left of the post office. They greeted us like old friends. The young and old played together along the riverbank, and the Spirit Thread kept them safe here on their journey to the hereafter.

It was Friday afternoon. The young men and boys had bought up the beer supply and were driving their Yamahas wildly up and down and around the streets. We walked up the steep slope to the general store, which was new and located at the top of the town.

The owner was a lady who had married an army man and lived many years in the famous GI housing in Levittown, Pennsylvania – the first such built for returning GIs. Her mother was from Ruby, so she had returned home. She probably made the better choice of the two places. Ruby's adults, her young, and her old were all in evidence. None were relegated to old folk homes, none to the nurseries. The young watched the old die. The old watched the young grow. In this way the Spirit Thread is never broken. The grandson in the river could not lose his way; the grandfather would see him 'Someplace.'

We purchased gas, Olympia beer at $16.00 a case, canned staples, and smoked salmon, and picked up our mail. We said goodbye to Ruby. A storm was brewing. Six miles down river, we located a sandbar south and directly across from Melozi Island. The place was low, wet, and shot full of black alders and bugs, but it was to be our home for the night.

Ken blessed the landing with Russian tea. Neill and I tossed a six pack of Olympia in the Yukon to cool. We talked and laughed about the large salmon I poked with my paddle leaving Ruby. I did not see him due to the silt in the river, and digging my paddle into the current I struck him. That dude really soaked me trying to escape by lunging from the river astern of *Pollux*. Jim started a fire, and we all pitched in to gather wood as Ken prepared supper. The meal was great. We ate fresh hamburger. It was a real treat to read letters from home about our Maryland, Virginia, Florida, and California families' various summer adventures. Tomorrow – westward to Galena.

Things began to happen on the 4th of August at 04:45. The pusher, *Romona II,* began her bump and grind around Big Island. She passed Melozi Island in front of the sun before Neill could photograph her. At 05:45 Ken left the tent. I followed at 06:00, and Jim saw the first light of day at 06:30. We followed our normal pattern and bid our bug ridden bar farewell at 08:05.

Shortly after we got on the river, we met an eastbound pusher, *Yukon*, of the Yukon Barge Fleet. We were caught in a narrow channel between Yuki Island and the high Sandstone Bluff, and were concerned because of the Yukon's wake. She was pushing three barges against a six to seven knot current, and she was applying plenty of horsepower in order to make headway. I told Ken to brace for some real haystacks. As I was saying this, the Yukon cut her speed, thus reducing her swell. The courtesy was one that one sailor extends to another and was greatly appreciated. As it was, we rode a good wake and bumped hydrostatic pressure swells for twenty minutes after exchanging salutes with the friendly, courteous pusher, *Yukon*.

We took fresh water from a freshet below Sandstone bluff on the right bank of the Yukon, and ate an early lunch east of Dainty Island. There we paused for a short weather break to allow a front to blow through. We left Dainty, bound for Fish Island bar, when we met several chaps in a welded hull, 100 horse, inboard/outboard Mercury, who wanted to talk about the condition of the river. They were out of Galena and bound for Ruby. They were nice guys who were connected with a small gold mining operation north of Ruby. They soon pushed on.

We pressed on westward toward Fish Island and the promise of a dry bar. We experienced shallow shoal water, wind, rain, and disappointment. Finally, we reached a dry sandbar, found freshwater, driftline firewood, and Sand Hill cranes – six of them – on a small bar south of our camp. We lucked out, in that we had our tents pitched and our gear stored under our weather fly minutes ahead of the major rain of the day.

Neill, Ken, and I drank our last few beers as we collected firewood and completed our camp chores. Night was fast approaching when we retired to the tents, and good weather was not going to prevail. It rained throughout the night, beating a tattoo on our nylon tents that varied in intensity as one snug hour wore into the next. At 01:30, I crawled out into a dark world and watched the running lights of an eastbound pusher as she searched for a safe passage through the north channel. I did not watch long, but attended to my immediate needs and returned to the shelter of the tent. I thought of the fish cannery that is under construction at Tanana, and considered that as the source of the increase in commerce on the lower Yukon River. If that cannery is to be completed, the supplies for such an operation will have to reach Tanana before the freeze up. Salmon have to be fished, canned and distributed before the next spring salmon run. The price of statehood runs high for Alaskans, and some we met along the Yukon were interested and willing to pay the bill. I returned to sleep, leaving such problems to those in the political and big business arena.

05:00 I got up. The gray of night fast fading was replaced by the dirty grays of a rainy dawn. The tattoo of rain continued on the tent. The camp slept, thankful for a day of rest. In my mind, I reviewed what I could remember of the lower Yukon: the fact that summer was fast fading at latitude 64°, 45' North; the endless day of the arctic and subarctic was being laced with interludes of night; and the probing fingers of cold began to be felt in the colder rains. The air cooled, and permafrost regained territory relinquished for a brief spell to the midnight sun. I thought of villages yet to be seen, such as Nulato, Kaltag, Grayling, Anvik, Holy Cross, Russian Mission, Marshall, and Andreafsky or Saint Mary's. I thought of how much we had learned about the caring people who watched after river travelers, their changing economy, their health care system, their ability to enjoy, not just survive, this frozen land as we paddled from east to west across the middle line playing along the Arctic Circle. The Brooks Range lay to the north of us, where John and his crew were already guiding winter hunters to the elusive Dall sheep and the fearful Grizzly. To the south of us lay the Tanana River, so filled with silt it was said the Tanana was "too thick to drink and too thin to cut." It carried the most commerce and helped bring a modicum of prosperity to the southern half of this state, which is twice the size of Texas.

Day arrived at Fish Island. Quietly the camp stirred. Fires were lighted, coffee served, and small talk started all in the rain. The order of routine makes for more relaxed camping. It is not easily broken.

09:00 we stripped the splash covers from *Castor* and *Pollux* and gave them a good bucket bath. We stashed rain soaked gear under the weather fly, and Neill did his sun dance. It failed. Rain fell, and Ken and I returned to the tent, she to read and I to my notes. The dark ominous clouds churned and rain tapped lightly on the tent. I soon slept. 11:30 hours Ken left her book and the tent. She was hungry. Soup was served at 12:00. She called me and I told her I would join soon. I was again working on my notes and did not want to leave. At 12:30 I came to eat and, for a change, clean the pots. By 13:00 hours, rain again fell. It was back to the tents. Dullsville.

The tent screen door zippers were now totally shot. Each tent had three doors: a fly screen, inner door, and rain door in the outer shell, all closing with zippers. Repairs were not possible due to the sodden condition of the fabric. Neither bugs nor weather can be controlled under these conditions. The question was, "can we solve our tent problem?" We faced a full river, high by Yukon standards, which reduced or totally eliminated many sandy points and bars by being flooded. This reduced our camping possibilities. Headwinds and rain had been our lot. As I reviewed these problems I realized none were yet unmanageable. I recorded them to take my mind off the continual rain that had followed us for fifty days on the river.

It rained all afternoon. Ken, bored with the day, fell asleep. Jim and Neill slept and snored in the second tent. At 15:00 I slipped out to scan the river for game with my binoculars, then fished until a heavier downpour sent me to cover under the fly. When the rain let up, I saved the fire. Ken joined me and we made Russian tea, a good picker-upper. We ate our Dinty Moore Stew bought in Ramps. We went to the shore for another drill practice with shotgun and rifle. Each member shot well. Day on Fish Island bar was done and filed in memory. Tomorrow we would paddle to Galena.

We joined around Jim's fire at 06:00 hours and left Fish Island for Bear Point, which we made handily by 09:00. The wind, waves, and slop proved troublesome, and yet the challenge of facing the resistance of wind and rain at upper levels coupled with the press of current at keel line proved exhilarating. We passed Bear Point. Louden Slough led to Bessy Slough, and once again to the broad expanse of the Yukon River. Galena was in sight. Cave Off Cliffs, rising 500 feet on the right hand at the water's edge, threatened us, and the strong beam seas were causing us to ride the current with bows pointing quarterwise at some of the large rollers. It appeared like we were canoeing backwards into Galena.

12:30 sharp, we landed at Galena and met Hobo, mayor, and self-proclaimed plenipotentiary, who, with twin brother Don, ruled all they surveyed – at least in Galena. Hobo was an ex-Michigan lad who had come to Galena in the Fifties and remained after his contract with the U.S. Air Force terminated. He was always willing to lend a hand to those who ventured down the Yukon. He had a friend with a Singer sewing machine who was willing to repair our tents. Only, she didn't know how to use it. Ken threaded the machine and sewed dress zippers in the weather fly. Once again we had dry tents for the 422 miles to reach Saint Mary's. We ate at the Galena Restaurant. We met Don, Hobo's twin brother and owner/operator of the liquor store. He was as clean-shaven and sober as Hobo was unshaven and inebriated. We went to Hobo's bar for drinks. At the door, a carved sign addressed the problem of fire arms in bars with the admonition: "All who enter here are subject to weapons search. If none are found, the establishment will loan you one."

Inside, painted on the mirror behind the bar, was a philosophical truth: *It is not he who has little, but he who wants more, who is poor.*

The population of Galena was about three hundred, and the home of Galena Air Force Base. There was a scheduled commercial air service between Galena and Fairbanks, and a charter service was available. All in all, Galena was more like a small town in the Lower Forties. It was a place to break our trip and to fly back to civilization. We chose to continue down river.

We departed Galena on a strong current to Serpentine Island, where we spent the night. It rained steadily throughout the night, testing Ken's handy work and trying our respective wills to reach Saint Mary's. It was during this storm I thought of the four hundred twenty-two miles we had yet to travel. I thought of the slower river and the map's promise of sluggish current and little in the way of scenery or points of interest. We would be canoeing through the largest migratory water birds flyway in the world. Great skeins of them were already in flight south.

Ken was the first to greet the 7th of August. Neill followed. Coffee ran third and I finally screwed up my courage to face the now familiar grays of the Alaskan mornings. I dressed in a tent that was sodden from the condensation of our body heat, due to the temperature differential between the inside and outside of the tent. If touched, it would start dripping. It became a challenge for us to dress without touching the tent walls, which were an arm's length in all directions. I felt good. I had spent thirty-three years of my life laboring in the vineyard so I could do what I was now doing. So why not enjoy that for which I had worked to achieve. First things first – feed the inner man! Rain be damned.

Breakfast was hot and good. We made ready to pack, and it began to drop great buckets of water from the heavens. It rained and rained. The day, one shower after continuous shower, tested our mettle. At 14:00 Ken and I crawled into the tent to sleep. At 15:00 the wet was unbearable. We left in time to view an east oncoming storm. We stood under our weather fly and laughed about Hobo's saloon sign. A Galena joke that helped put everyone in good humor.

Our happy hour at 17:00 was a relief. We drank Russian tea and ate saltine crackers in the rain. We snapped the splash covers securely to the boats. They provided some protection for our cargo, and relieved us of pulling all the gear from the canoes at each campsite. As Neill and I worked with the snaps, we talked of the distance left on our journey and questioned the possibility of success, especially in the face of the extreme weather we were experiencing, which was proving to be a continuing challenge. We resolved to continue our trip; and make it we would, barring severe weather and storms on the ever widening Yukon, with its high mud banks, dwindling fire wood, and slow but strong current.

A little chap wearing his brown summer suit with a black tipped tail demanded our immediate attention. He enlivened our midday by bounding around our camp in the rain. He and his girlfriend were racing around our tent and stopping at the corners for a frolic in the sand. They continued to entertain us throughout the night. He ran flat out on the straight way, throwing dirt against the corners of the blue nylon in his haste to complete the circle. She squeaked either approval, or disapproval, of his efforts. The two lovers were weasels. Their color changed, with the onset of winter, from brown to white – while continuing to wear their black tail tips – and become known as ermine.

At 04:00 the skies were gray with the promise of water yet to fall. Will the rain never end? I returned to the tent and a short fitful sleep. By 05:30 a new day was born, proving just how fickle the Alaskan weather can be as one works from the higher elevation of Lake Laberge down the long slide that eventually ends at the Bering Sea. Laberge, with an elevation of 2,060 feet, provides the energy for the Yukon, flowing down the western side of the Rockies in its race to the sea. It was quite a sleigh ride.

As we packed, I looked in vain for our little ermine. They were nowhere to be found. By dawn, they had exhausted themselves and were under some pile of driftwood asleep. We bid the Serpentine adieu at 08:20 hours.

We slipped north across the Yukon and made straight for Jimmy's Slough, which we made in a handy manner. Hen and Cat Islands were on our right, and Pilot Mountain Slough slipped past our laboring canoes. Shortly thereafter, the Yukon bellied to the north, then did a column's left with a skid, a roil, and one hell of a whirl. Bishop Rock, with its beautiful cross marking the final resting place of Bishop Bompas of the Anglican Church, rushed by to port, as did the small Indian village of Yistletow.

Lunch was enjoyed on Bishop Rock Island, then we were off east-northeast down the Bishop Rock Slough. Whontleya lay on our north hand. Koyakuk Island passed to starboard, and then the village of Koyakuk popped into view. We did not enter. By 15:30 we took drinking water on the north bank from a small stream directly across the river from Mogotsol Island. We spoke with several Indians who were in the process of smoking fish for their winter food. They invited us to spend time with them, but we were forced to hurry on. A great storm appeared to be brewing, and we were interested in making camp before we were caught in heavy weather. We reached Gemodedon Island where, due to shallow water on the head bar, we had to fight our way ashore by long-lining the canoes over the sand.

On the morning of the 8th, I awakened with a start, realizing with a flash that we had missed the Last Chance liquor store. Hobo had told us to be sure to stop for replenishment of our supplies. I had seen a large two-story log building up a short slough the previous day, but did not give it a second thought. I guess it was brought to mind by last night's visitors, three sodden Indians at 22:00 hours. They arrived noisily, hitting the bar outside our island home with a mighty crash. The crash, followed by obscenities, announced visitors. Short minutes later, the trio, who had great difficulty in walking, descended on Neill's tent and were promptly sent packing. The Indians departed, using some of the more colorful Anglo-Saxon words learned, not from their cradle, but from our cradle of civilization.

I had a good laugh at 05:00 as I viewed the footprints in the sand and thought of last night's visitors. We built a huge fire. The sun shone. We all felt good, completed our morning chores, and departed at 07:45. What a day! Even the north wind was in our corner, and all was right with the world.

09:45 we landed at Nulato, checked for mail, shopped for groceries in a very neat, orderly small store, collected our purchases, and departed. Nulato was the site of the first settlement made by white men on the Yukon River. The Russians built a trading post there in 1838. This post was later attacked and burned by Indians in 1851. Nulato today is an Indian village with an airstrip and intermittent service to Fairbanks. It is a quiet little town with a dark and deadly past.

As we pushed off down river, the sun shone and the northeast breeze rode the quarterdecks of *Castor* and *Pollux*. The day saw our canoes slide past Big Island and several unnamed islands. Halfway Island, west of Nine Mile River where we fished for pike, held fish camps. Below Halfway Island we landed on Seven Mile Island bar following a beautiful river run of thirty-nine miles. We had a few drinks and another freeze-dried supper.

As night fell, Neill and I sat around our fire and watched five separate rain squalls play on the horizon. The wind freshened north-northeast and a storm became evident. Ken was safe in the tent with her notes. In my opinion the measure, in truth, of a real outdoor gal, and one whom it is a pleasure to travel and canoe with.

CHAPTER IX
The Williwaw, The Bear, and Northern Hospitality

06:00 hours on August 10th, I left the tent to face mosquitoes and start the morning campfire. Ken prepared breakfast, fed the crew, packed the kitchen, and helped load the boats. We departed at 09:00 for Kaltag, nine miles west.

We arrived in Kaltag at 11:10. A young Indian met and walked with us to Ed Kalland's grocery store, where he introduced us to Mr. and Mrs. Kallands, who were manning the store. Their store looked like the old country grocery stores seen in many small towns in the Lower Forties during the depression of the thirties. In the south, these stores were a vital part of the economy until after World War II. The store was well stocked with pharmacy products and school supplies, as well as groceries. We bought canned meats, stews, vegetables, big Alaskan onions, potatoes, pickled bologna, Red River cereal, bread, eggs, soap, paper towels, matches, peanut butter, and Milky Way and Mounds candy bars. Rats, no more Sweet Maries.

At seventy-five years of age, Ed was still full of life and busy in the community as one of its leaders. He and his wife were as congenial hosts as we had met. We spent more than an hour listening to Ed tell of his years as a pusher skipper on the Yukon River. He warned us to watch the sky and listen for the loud south windstorms called williwaws. They were violent and quick passing, leaving many a drifter on the bottom of the Yukon.

"Because of these storms," he said, "do not canoe the middle of the river. Stay close to the shore so you can easily and quickly land." On our departure, Ed walked to the high riverbank with us. There he sat with a camera as we four "drifters," which he termed us, passed his vantage point. He photographed *Castor* and *Pollux* with their crews paddling down the river. Ken, with our Binocamera, photographed Ed.

At 12:30 hours we ate lunch. The sun was full and the day still. We returned to the boats, but the day was too gorgeous. We needed a bath, and agreed to check the bars on Little and Big Eight Mile Island for a campsite. 14:30 we arrived at Big Eight Mile Island, landed, beached the boats, made camp, and called it home, twenty-one miles below Kaltag.

Campen Fish Camp near Eight Mile Island below Kaltag. This is a typical fish drying operation, seen at many places along the banks of the Yukon.

Drinks were served at 15:30, and by 16:00 we were happy we had listened to Mr. Kallands. We experienced our first encounter with a williwaw. First we heard what sounded like a freight train. Looking south down river, we saw a dark sheet of rain whipping surface water before it into a madman's fury. Our weather fly, filled with the press of wind, raised from the ground tie-down logs that we three men had worked hard to move into place. We looked to see if our tent ties were holding. The tents looked like big "U"s with their storm sides pressed to their lea sides. A solid wall of rain charged up the center of the river, pushing destruction to all things not secured or out of its way. It hardly seemed wider than the two mile river and its immediate shorelines. Hail followed in its wake. We were soaked, but thankful to be on our bar, to have our gear safe, and to have been warned by Ed Kallands. The storm raced up the Yukon to the north and peace returned to our camp. Lear Point, two and one-half miles north of camp, which had been completely eclipsed during the williwaw, appeared again. We said good night to the world and retired. It was also good night to the 55th day of our journey.

The sound of an early morning campfire is good. It is especially pleasing when your ear tells you it is burning well. I left the tent to find both Jim and Neill warming by the result of their efforts. Ken followed me into a gray leaden morning. We stood by a huge fire, drank black coffee, and watched helplessly as our plans for the day slowly dripped away with the rain.

First, the mountains to the west were eradicated by heavy black clouds that blotted out the panorama. To the south and north, rain like billowing white smoke eliminated the landscape. To the east, a small patch of sunlight flashed briefly on an unnamed mountaintop, then some unseen hand removed the mountain from view. The wind flowed south to southwest, and kept us dancing around the fire to avoid the smoke. Rain fell on Big Eight Mile Island. I closed my mind to travel and returned to the tent. Ken soon followed. Once out of the storm, Ken read and I worked over the remaining charts and wrote. Neill and Jim suffered under the weather fly until boredom chased them to their tent to read or sleep. In my tent, I thought of the three hundred and thirty-eight miles to St. Mary's and the fact that the way was fraught with sandbars, bugs, mud, and williwaws. Mix these ingredients with an ever widening, cold river and you have a situation no novice should try to handle. Indeed, the Yukon is no river to trifle with or to take lightly. She represents challenge in every mile, and the price of misjudgment can be injury, loss of boats, and possibly of life itself. Ed Kallands knew this all too well. He had lost to the river friends who were far more knowledgeable than ourselves. I silently thanked him again for his advice about williwaws.

At noon, the sky, still heavy with rain and wind streaked, worsened and warned us to stay off the river. Grudgingly we listened. We ate a heavy noon meal with the intent of taking advantage of the first possible weather break. By 15:00, such a break had not arrived. We talked things over, and decided to stay camped on Big Eight Mile Island bar. We washed clothes and did camp chores. We collected fire wood under our weather fly, long lined the canoes to the tree line where we moored them, tightened the splash covers, and rigged the camp for more storm assaults from the west. We dried wet laundry on dingle sticks around our fire. We had coffee, and ate potatoes and onion fried with a can of hash.

At 19:30 hours, a beautiful rainbow appeared on the east bank, and a large skein of wild geese crossed the Yukon on their way south to a warmer winter. The skein of geese was our first indication winter would soon visit the northland. We retired to our tents to read, write, and get out of the weather. Inside we were warm and dry. We settled to our self-assigned tasks and, Lo and Behold, it rained.

Around 21:00, Ken left the tent to secure some gear under the weather fly. She returned in a hurry asking in an excited voice to be let into the tent as soon as possible. I let her in just as our old friend the williwaw pounced on our camp like a cat on a mouse. The sound of rushing wind, the flapping nylon of our weather fly, the luffing of splash covers, and the shriek of lines made ever taut by the rising wind created a cacophony of discord. Inside the tents we were dry and warm, although the dimensions of our small quarters were distorted by the extreme pressure of the howling wind and storm. It was like finding oneself sealed in a ribbed envelope then pressed flat by a great invisible weight. Within a quarter of an hour, the storm passed on north up the Yukon to conquer other locations. As it did, we left our shelters to review the damage. Nothing serious, but thank the good Lord for Ed Kallands, who put himself in the right place at the right time to protect four drifters ignorant of the deadly williwaws.

Again, it rained most of the night of August 12th, at times heavily. Inside, our tents sounded like snare drums. At 01:30, I crawled out to check on things in general. All was well, but I felt a growing concern for the soon to come daylight. The idea of spending another of our fast disappearing weather days on an island had little appeal. By 05:50 I was up. Neill had the fire jumping. We stood by the burning logs and talked of pushing on as we stared into the red embers of the fire. The day was calm; the storms of last night had vanished. We ate, packed our gear, and were on the river by 07:30. Things were going good.

We took fresh water from a small stream on the west bank just below our home of yesterday. The boats were in step and moving at a good pace when Ken took gas (so to speak). A deadhead is a submerged obstruction in the river. This one was a log that had one end lodged in the river bottom, which allowed its head to bob up and down with the current. You can't see it until its head bobs to the surface, which it did just as Ken was dipping her paddle into the water. It bumped the stern of our canoe as we passed by, barely missing our keel, which would have dumped us in the river. It could have done severe damage to our thin hull, and quite possibly to our rapidly thinning selves.

Lunch was served on Quail Island's head bar. The sun shone. Thirty minutes later, black clouds covered the sun. We returned to the boats and ran the lea side of Quail Island out of the real weather for six miles. When we reached the island's end, we crossed to the west bank through severe turbulence caused by the combination of swift current and strong wind. It was not the type of crossing one forgets, and it was not the type one would recommend, but it had to be done. By 14:15 we landed on a small noname sandbar, happy to be dry and on solid footing. Camp was set, and Ken counted our day's work at twenty-six miles. She retired to the tent after serving hot Russian tea and – you're right – it rained.

By late afternoon the storm passed, and Ken emerged from her blue cocoon. It was time for supper. We ate in near silence as we watched black clouds form in the east. We knew it was time to go to the tents, but we waited until the first big drops landed with a splat on the weather fly above us. "Goodnights" were yelled as we four raced, with hot coffee in hand, to the security of our tents. Once inside, with the door zipped tight, we heard a Sand Hill Crane land near the tent and scold as he looked over the large blue and green egg-shaped intruders on his island. In the distance, on yet another bar, a lone gull complained at being a displaced person. Rain cut short the lonely sounds of the subarctic, and peace returned to the Alaskan wilderness. As Charles Kuralt would have said, "It happened that way three hundred and fifteen miles east of Saint Mary's."

On the 13th of August, our 58th day on the river, daylight came on quiet feet and stood in silence as the Yukon flowed noisily past our island. Neill, the first to rise, had a good fire going. Soon the four of us gathered to enjoy hot coffee and the fire and to examine the morning. One thing was certain – this would be a good day to travel. How far? Who knows? Only the Alaskan weather and the good Lord held the answer to that.

In the east, a few streaks of sun held forth a promise, while the north held the gray prisoner. The west hugged wind streaks and gray billowing clouds along the horizon. The southern cardinal point passed. We packed our gear and removed our shoes and socks so we could better float the canoes to a depth where we could safely board them. By 08:00 we were in our canoes, putting socks and shoes on wet, cold feet and getting underway.

The morning remained calm and the miles melted with the hours. Eagle Slide and Bull Frog Island passed, the latter to port. Tip Top Mountain marked our progress as it stood on our starboard hand. We gathered fresh water from a spring, and Ken added to her collection a new flower we could not classify. At 11:45, in the face of a brisk breeze from the south, we paused for lunch. The place we chose was south of Jensen Creek Slough on the west bank of the Yukon. A pack of sled dogs, chained to posts driven along the riverbank in Indian fashion, took note of our arrival, provided a wilderness serenade, then stood silent as we passed their assigned duty stations and landed south of their location.

As we ate lunch, I expressed concern over the change in the weather. Eagle Island, three miles south and in the middle of the river, presented a mile of open water in front of her head bar. The wind had stiffened, and that mile was covered with whitecaps and curlers. That mile, as I viewed it, was no place for my crew. We held a brief conference and it was agreed we would wait out the wind.

We stood around an open fire for two hours, helpless. We watched two Indians with heavy outboards push a raft of logs and firewood slowly down the river in the very teeth of the wind. At 14:00 we drowned our fire, relaunched our boats, and took one last fling at the river. Our effort fell short. Our progress was one more mile. We quit. The wind did not lessen, and I would not put a boat into that gale in open water. Camp was set amid bugs and mud. We ate and retired early to save some of our skin for the bugs for the coming day. May the winds of the Yukon follow our example.

At 21:30 we listened as an outboard motor coughed and died near our canoes. A "Hello" brought me from the tent, followed by Ken and later, Neill. We had visitors. Rick Freireich from Grayling and his wife, Josephine, paid a call. We sat around a dying fire in a cold drizzly rain. As we visited, Josephine put small sticks on the red coals to help maintain what was left of the heat. Rick, originally from Cleveland, Ohio, had lived in Alaska six years. He and Josephine had two small sons. Josephine's father was the Athabascan Chief, John Deacon, who lived in Grayling. The Freireichs were on their way to Eagle Slide to cut firewood for the winter when they spotted our camp and stopped to talk.

Josephine said, "The last time we went for wood we were chased out by a bear. We stayed three days longer than we had told Father we would be. Mother keeps our two boys. They worry about us. Rick will always be a greenhorn in Father's eyes."

Rick chimed in, "Stop in Grayling and tell them you have seen us, that we will be home in five days. Stop by our fish wheel and take a salmon with you."

They bade us goodbye and headed upriver in their outboard. This ended our 58th day on the Yukon with new friends, a funny bear story, and a message to take to John Deacon.

We knew that by their visit we were incorporated into the famous bush ptarmigan telegraph, a system that allows all on the river to learn, in a very rapid manner, the news that effects their river and locality. But mostly, it keeps families in touch with each other. It is news carried by word of mouth, and those entrusted with it are considered part of the entire river system. We were honored to be accepted by river people as river travelers of some note, and people to be trusted. The Freireichs' visit had not been happenstance. They had expected to see us *someplace* on their way up river.

The 14th of August, our 59th day on the Yukon, saw a canoe run of eighteen miles. We awakened at 05:30 to watch the sky as we drank our morning coffee. The day was heavy and dull, with a vague hint of weather. 07:45 we were on the river. We wanted miles and were willing to purchase them with lots of paddle work.

Our boats hurried down the channel west of Eagle Island on a rather placid river. By 10:30 we needed a break, so we entered Wood Creek. The wind had risen and a light chop was on the Yukon. The wind blew from the south, making our day difficult. As we rested on the bank of Wood Creek, Jim, a real fisherman,

saw several fish jump. They were feeding. We quickly boarded
Castor and *Pollux* and slipped up Wood Creek to try our luck.
Within thirty minutes, we collected eight 12" to 16" white fish.
We returned to the mouth of the creek to check on the condition
of the river. It was rough, but the wind appeared to be letting up,
so we determined to quit play and return to the serious work the
river had set before us. I quickly cleaned the fish, stored the
fishing gear, and departed the Wood Creek-Yukon River estuary
with our cleaned fish stuck in a bucket under my seat. Rounding
the point, we felt the increased intensity of the wind. The Yukon,
a wide river at that point, was covered with rollers and whitecaps
that lashed up river and over the strong flowing current. Travel
was impossible. We returned to the shelter of the creek to await
a change in weather. We waited nine hours around an open fire
for such a change to happen. As we waited, we pulled the Coleman
stove from *Pollux*. I filleted the fish and Ken cooked them for
early supper. We repacked our gear following our evening meal,
knowing we could not spend the night on Wood Creek. The area,
a high mud bank full of logs and rocks, had barely enough flat
area for our stove – definitely none for tents. 20:00 hours, the
wind died and the sea abated. We immediately left for Blackburn
Island, where our maps indicated we would find a good sandbar.
We hoped our maps were right this time, as rivers, especially
large rivers in the north, change with every season. The questions always before us were, "What will be the condition of our
next camp? Are the maps reliable? Will the place be dry enough
for tents? What about water and bugs? What about those vicious
little no-see-ums? Will they greet us and eat us? You bet. Last
but not least, will we find wood for our fire?"

At 22:30, darkness began to gather and a red gold sun sat in
the west, turning our world into a thing of solitary beauty. We
beached our canoes on Blackburn Island. The maps were right,
the sandbar was there, and what a bar it was. There were miles
and miles of sandbars. We were but small specks, perched on the
black alder edge near the majestic river. We set camp and retired, thankful for our island, and happy to be in the subarctic

stillness away from the howling wind that had made our day such a long vigil.

At 02:30, I awakened to the howling of at least six different wolves, all directing their lament at a partial moon. I thought, "This is Alaska – this is worth the effort." I returned to sleep not knowing that Ken, too, was listening beside me to the solitude and lonesome serenade in the cold Alaskan night that represented the prelude to coming winter.

August 15th we were up at 05:30. Ken left the tent and jammed the zipper on the weather door. I was trapped and lost my cool. It didn't last. It never does. I can't stay angry about anything for a long period. I sputtered a little, sprung myself and headed for the canoes. I had yesterday's last and largest fish to fillet. Jim joined me, and we finished the job. Ken had the skillet hot, and quickly turned the fish to a rich, golden brown tasty meal. We had plenty for breakfast.

By 08:00, we were off Blackburn Island with a light following breeze and a calm Yukon. If the weather holds throughout the day we will make miles. We soon passed an unusually neat cabin on the site of the once small village of Blackburn. Our map stated that the village was abandoned. It was just not there where it was supposed to be located. By 09:50 we stopped on the bank west of Alice Island. We were doing well. We paused for lunch on the east bank north of Saint Joe Creek and south of Alice Island. The Yukon's current ran hard as we pushed from the west to the east bank of the river, which was a good three quarters of a mile wide and rushing toward the sea. The east bank appeared on the map to be drier land, which we needed for a campsite.

After lunch and a chance to warm at the midday fire, we moved on, passing unnamed sandbars, islands, and high cut banks. We headed for Simon Point as the day began to change. Gray clouds and light rain took command of the river. We were forced off three miles north of Fox Point Island. Wild wind, rain, and the threat of a williwaw ended our run of twenty-eight miles and put a finishing touch to our 60th day on the Yukon.

Prior to retiring, we reviewed the maps, noting that we would, weather permitting, reach Grayling about midday. From Grayling it is roughly two hundred and fifty miles to Saint Mary's and the end of the trail. I suppose each of us could not help feeling a little sad at the prospect of bringing our journey to an end, because we had developed a real attachment for the Yukon, its fickle weather, but especially its affable people.

Our 61st day broke with a scattered gray cloud system and a fresh northeast breeze. We ate breakfast and hurried with packing. 08:00 we were on the river, headed for Grayling, approximately fifteen miles south of our position. We cleared the point of the bar by 08:15 and set our course for Fox Point Island's west channel. 09:15 we stopped at a small glacial stream at the southern end of the island on the west bank for fresh water. We hurried through our task and returned to the main body of the river. We were making good time.

Rounding the high headland south of Fox Point Island, we rode a strong current past the sight of the small Kokrines Bible School. No one appeared except a large black bear walking the shore searching for his breakfast. He found medium sized white fish, which he deftly slipped from the river. I swung *Pollux* and bore down on him. My bowman, cook, chief mate (really skipper), and fish netter grabbed her camera. I yelled and Blackie posed, fish in mouth and a "Who the heck are you looking at?" He stepped into high grass, sat like a large dog eating his catch, and dared us to come ashore and further disturb him. We slipped quietly down river and caught up with Neill and Jim, glad and we could so easily leave the old boy to his breakfast.

Eagle Island, the second by that name, came into view and passed to port. We were fast closing on Grayling, but not before I spotted another bear near a fish wheel. He moved into the alders before we could photograph him. Eleven sharp we beached our boats at Grayling, noting as we did some clever soul had removed the 'G R' from the village name and the 'A' from Alaska.

Following our landing, we visited the Post Office and native store. We picked up the six Milky Ways they had left and an-

other jar of peanut butter. We delivered Rick and Josephine's
message to her parents, the John Deacons.

John and Elsa Deacon were Athabascan leaders in their tribe.
He was the Chief that made all the decisions effecting the welfare of his people in Alaska. John was ninety years young. Elsa
was his third wife and considerably younger. As John's wife, she
was influential in the social scheme of Grayling, and the welfare
of all its citizens. They lived in a large two story home, the only
two story house in Grayling. The home was fenced with chain
link. John's wealth was considerable, having earned it in the fur
trade and gold mines.

They invited us into their living room for a visit. We sat on
an old overstuffed sofa. To Ken's left was a large potted palm.
The anachronism was soon explained when Elsa told us Rick's
parents lived in Florida. Rick and Florence's two sons, three and
four year olds, stood by their grandmother. They wore cowboy
hats and boots and Elsa's hands politely placed in front of the
boy parts. The boys and their parents had recently returned from
Florida visiting Rick's parents. The boys called themselves half
Indian and half American. The Deacons had an extended family,
although the exact number of children was not known. A shy
young daughter came down the stairs to say hello and quickly
disappeared. John, Jr. was married and lived nearby in the village. John, Sr. had helped Rick build a log cabin last year. He
and Elsa laughed, recounting Rick's ineptness with tools. Then
it was our turn to tell them about us, although they already knew
a lot from the news that travels ahead of strangers on the Yukon.

John was surprised to learn we had started our trip at
Whitehorse on June 17th. His eyes lit up as we told about our
struggles with the constant rain. He reveled in listening to us
telling about our problems, as it recalled his experiences with the
river. In his mind's eye, he joined our venture and was in full
accord with our undertaking, for he was an old river hand, who
knew, trusted, and respected the Yukon and its tributaries. They
had provided his livelihood in the Alaskan wilderness. Our visit
ending, The Chief insisted we take a fish from his wheel, which

was located just below our canoes.

We returned to the canoes and made ready to depart. John, Jr. had come to the canoes to say goodbye and offer us a fish from the family's fish wheel for supper. Rick and Josephine had also extended the invitation when they were at our camp. With everyone in agreement on the gift of fish, we thanked John and pushed off in our canoes.

Grayling was a modern town with its streets laid out in blocks and well oiled to settle the dust. It was far from "ailing" as the sign that greeted us implied. Fifteen minutes south of Grayling we came alongside the Deacon-Freireich fish wheel. Ken climbed out on the box and peered in, but if she were the only one to pick out fish we would go hungry. Ken returned to hold the canoe steady in the strong current, while I climbed aboard the box to get a fish. It required much longer arms than Ken had. The box had about five hundred pounds of fish in it and was less than half full. Ken reminded me of her struggle to cook a 34lb. salmon on the four burner, so I took her advice, selected a small silver salmon, and reboarded the canoe. We were once more off down river.

Lunch on the west bank was a quick affair heavily laced with black gnats. The gnats gave us plenty of incentive to move on. We wanted miles and the river was waiting.

15:00 we landed on a sandbar approximately six miles north of Anvik. Anvik was the farthest fort up river that the Russians had settled. It rained as we set up camp. I cleaned our salmon in the river, filleted it, and turned the real work over to Kenny. Once again we ate a supper that was a gourmet delight. We stood for a long period watching the rain fall in and around our fire, and listened to it hit on the weather fly that was rigged to offer the maximum of protection from the elements. We watched Neill run streams off its edge, collecting the rain in our water skins. Finally, we drifted to our tents saying our goodnights as we went. We were all tired from our day's labor on the river, and happy to be quiet and warm and out of the rain. We were not yet ready for sleep, so we settled to our own projects. Ken to writing, and me to nothing other than thoughts of our day in Grayling – especially our visit with the Deacons, their gift of a fresh salmon, and northern hospitality. Tomorrow we would continue southward on the Yukon, weather permitting.

05:30 came early. We left the tent and faced a wind-streaked sky. Things did not add up to travel, at least at 05:30 hours. I started a fire, wet wood and all. The batting order for the morning was Ken, Neill, and Jim a poor third. Jim did not make muster until 07:00. By that hour the heavens had not made up the day's schedule. The wind flawed and one small front after another marched through our camp. We ate breakfast and changed the rigging on our weather fly, bracing for a strong southwest to south wind. Yesterday evening we had rigged for a north to northeast blow that came, and during the night departed. By 08:00 the clouds floated over the near mountains and the sun shown briefly. Perhaps a good day that had gotten off to a bad start was in the making.

We dismantled camp and packed out at 08:55. We were no sooner off our sandbar home when 'the wheel came off.' The wind blew hard from the south, driving heavy swells with white-cap curlers north over the strong running current of the Yukon. *Castor*, driving her bow into the swells, took water over her forecomb. We quartered the seas that tossed buckets of whitewater over our splash cover and back into the river. Swinging our stern to the wind, we met the current head on. Our backs became sails, supplying the power that sent us rapidly to the small, wet, bug-ridden bar where we landed. *Castor* followed close behind. It was 09:30. Total time on the Yukon: thirty-five minutes. It seemed like weeks.

Once on shore, we lit a small fire, not finding enough wood to support a larger one. We had to reach the west bank of the river, where we could see plenty of dry driftwood. Neill and Jim were cold and wet. *Castor* had shipped a lot of water.

The wind quieted and we quickly relaunched the boats. The river, a half mile wide at this point, had more bounce to the ounce than Pepsi Cola, but we made the crossing and beached on a high stony point north of the vertical Hawk Bluff cliffs below Anvik.

We collected wood and made a large fire that dried and warmed all of us. To kill time, we ate lunch, slept on the ground, talked, and waited for another weather change. The day was shot. Our average number of miles per day was shot, and our estimated time of arrival at Saint Mary's in jeopardy. What were we doing about the situation? Playing the waiting game with the fickle weather.

All day long, the wind blew and the seas ran high on the open water beyond the cliffs of Anvik. We sat by our boats near an open fire, and for pastime walked to a small stone covered point to watch the progress of the weather and the condition of the river beyond the high cliffs. By 17:00 it was apparent the wind was growing tired of toying with us and would soon grow still. We ate an early supper, packed our gear, and at 18:00 left the cliffs of Anvik. The current ran fair and strong. The swells were diminishing. Seven miles passed rapidly. Anvik and Hawks Bluff were far astern.

As we rode the current roils of the river, I thought of future travelers on the Yukon and of our experience with the Alaskan south winds of August. My advice: "Beware." One should keep in mind that the Anvik River is about one and three-quarter miles north of Anvik. The village is connected with the river by a slough. The combination river mouth and slough offers safe haven from the south and west wind storms, and provides access to the village. All the river villages are located on sloughs that protect them from the rages of the uncontrollable Yukon River.

At 19:30 hours we were riding a strong current. Fish wheels and gill nets passed by, as did Slim Island. We landed on a mud and sand bar four miles below Hawks Bluff, pulled our boats to dry ground through tons of mud, and made a quick camp for the night. The gnats and no-see-ums attacked in swarms and made life miserable. We appreciated the protection offered by the fly and bug netting of our small tents and Deep Woods Off bug spray – especially effective on the no-see-ums at our outdoor bathrooms.

Our 62nd day on the river provided an eight hour wind bound trip with a net gain of twelve river miles. It was a real experience, and one we were certain would repeat itself, for we were faced with two hundred and thirteen miles of wide river before we would reach Saint Mary's. The effects of the Alaskan fall were in evidence, not only in the landscape but also in the weather. Time was not working to our advantage.

The 18th of August registered with each of us at 06:00. We arose and were greeted by an ominous day. The east held streaks of cold light. To the south, storm clouds shoved and pushed each other along the horizon, and yet the Yukon remained calm with the exception of current flaws and a few small cat paws. We ate breakfast and packed out. We wanted miles to make up for yesterday's losses. By 08:30 we were launched and sitting in the boats cleaning mud from our bare feet before putting on shoes and manning our paddles.

We settled to the routine of paddling, happy to be underway. We spotted large skeins of Canada Geese on the south end of our bar. They took to the air with a rush of wings and loud chatter as we approached. It was an impressive to see hundreds of wild geese in the gray rolling Alaskan sky. We were canoeing through the largest waterfowl breeding grounds in the world.

By 08:45 we cleared our bar and headed for Elk Horn Island to the south. The wind awakened and blessed us with stiff resistance. The river began to show teeth. We were surrounded by slop and chop. *Castor* and *Pollux* bobbed and weaved, ducked and lunged as they labored on the wind tossed Yukon. 10:00 hours we were abeam of Bonesila River, which enters the Yukon from the west. We were cold and wind blown, so we stopped and lit a fire. We cut room in the thick alders as a protection, of sorts, from rain. By 10:30 we were so blessed. We ate lunch and watched for a weather break.

At noon, the wind changed and the rain slackened. We launched our boats with full knowledge that our break was only a lull in the storm. The southern horizon was leaden and streaked with wind that had not yet reached us. Our temporary shelter was too wet and offered no room for tents, or we would never have ventured again on the river.

We cleared the river mouth and the wind jumped us – a strong headwind that soon made heavy seas over a fast current. The going was rough. We struggled on, passing Bonasila Slough and holding our heading on Cement Hill, a stone cliff of vertical rock that rose 250 feet from the water's edge north of Carlos Island. The wind increased in force and tortured the Yukon, and the Yukon fought back, throwing its mighty current into the very teeth of the gale, causing the wind to shriek and lash at the river. By 14:00 we were wet and wind tossed. We spotted Turtle Island with its sand head bar.

We quit. Four hours of rough water with a net gain of nine miles to show for our effort was too much. We pulled our boats high and dry among a myriad of bear tracks and geese droppings. We set camp in the rain in one of Nature's rookeries. This one was for geese. The bar looked like a barnyard, with the grass eaten to root level and dappled with droppings; but it was flat and dry, and we were off the raging river. We drank hot Russian tea under our weather fly and listened to the rattle of rain and the low growl and roar of high seas on the surface of the Yukon, which was still full of wind and fury. Overhead, skeins of geese fought the wind and scolded the intruders on their bar below. As we watched the storm, a black bear appeared across the slough from our tent, searching the shoreline for salmon. The luffing and popping of our weather fly sent him back into the alders.

During supper we talked of the sign on our bar. Without effort, we had seen grizzly tracks, moose and geese droppings, and sign of mink, muskrat, beaver, and wolves. The search for sign of all these animals kept us busy and entertained albeit frustrated, in that the tracks and sign were seen, but not the birds and animals that had made them. We had felt all the wind and rain we wanted, which finally sent us to our tents early. Before sleep closed the day, we checked our log. We were ending our 63rd day on the river. The maps pointed firmly to the fact that we had two hundred and four miles to cover before we would reach St. Mary's.

CHAPTER X
Turtle Island to Holy Cross

Turtle Island was our 54th camp, and it proved to be a lasting one. It rained all through the night. The wind never let up gusting south by east and south. Rain fell in sheets, pelting our tents like falling shot and creating a cacophonous sound within. Sleep proved elusive, perhaps because of the early hour at which we retired last evening. We were dry and warm. Somehow Ken slept. In the second tent someone snored. I knew all was well there.

04:00 hours I crawled out into the dark. The world was wet. A fine mist-like fog drifted into my face from the southwest. The wind, still puffy, had shifted. Perhaps by daylight we will see fair weather. I returned to the warmth of the tent as a steady rain began to fall. Shortly after the hour of 05:00, I awakened to the sound of an ax. Jim was up and feeding the fire. I joined him. Together we cut wood. Neill appeared and began dragging our product to the fire. Ken met the day with her "Good Morning," and being our aerographer, began to analyze the weather. West: wind. East: clear. Clouds: nimbus. Chance of more wind and rain: good to excellent. Was she rubbing it in? Then, as if the gods of weather were listening, rain like smoke descended on Turtle Island.

We stood under our nylon fly drinking hot coffee and rationalizing our position. Two hundred and four miles to St. Mary's was not bad. Nine days on the paddles with good weather should see us off the river. On the other hand, we covered only twenty-one miles in the last two days. Not good. We should have traveled fifty. Should we attempt to travel today? Not in this rain. We ate breakfast. Rain fell. It was Sunday. We four crept into our tents. Devil take the weather.

At noon, the wind fell and a weak sun poked through the clouds. We heard the piper's tune and danced along. We ate a quick lunch and decamped. We were on the river at 13:55 hours headed for Cement Hill, a high vertical rock formation that looked like the bow of a ship jutting out into the Yukon. It blocked all effort to see around it. We cleared Turtle Island seeking a lea in the shadow of Cement Hill. We were making reasonable progress toward it when a wind from the south hit the Yukon. The piper piped his tune, but we did not follow. I called the tune. We turned our boats and crept along the high vertical cliffs short of the headland. The seas began to run north over a strong south bound current and in no time were three to four feet high carrying whitecaps on their crests. They formed haystacks, out of control, steep and dangerous. We inched *Castor* and *Pollux* around in step with the driving swells, and eased into the channel that ran behind Turtle Island.

Once safe inside the channel, we looked back on the main body of the Yukon. She was a wild fury. The wind pushed us back against the current faster than we had been able to paddle with the current five minutes ago. We were blown back to the campsite we had left less than two hours earlier. God was looking out for fools and old sailors, or the Yukon wasn't in need of four more bodies, for we could not have survived the fury of that quick subarctic storm.

By 15:30 we beached our boats thankful to be on solid ground. We threw more wood on still warm ashes buried in the mineral soil. We reset the camp, had hot Russian tea, and crawled into our tents. We were warm and dry once more as we lay on our ground mats listening to the relentless struggle of wind, current and water clashing and smashing on our bar and across a wide, wild river.

Again I began to assess our position. It was obvious we were trapped in Alaska's autumnal storms. It was clear that this had been a warmer than usual summer causing excessive glacial melt as well as a wet summer creating the flood-like conditions on the Yukon. Also certain was the impending end of autumn and then freeze up. The nights had grown longer followed by days with patchwork weather that was wild and restless with wind, rain and unexpected williwaws. The map indicated we were approximately twenty-four miles north of Holy Cross, where we could obtain more specific weather information, and where, if the situation dictated, we might obtain charter transportation to Fairbanks. It just might be that Alaska's weather and the possible onset of early winter, not the Yukon, would defeat us. It was still two hundred and four miles to St. Mary's and we were again weather bound and weary.

Throughout the long night of August 19th, the rain pounded our small tents. A savage wind tugged and tore at them as if it were trying to destroy the last vestige of their existence. Toward the early hours of morning, I lay in a half-sleep wondering just how much punishment our frail Jansports could endure. Structurally they were fine. It was the nylon zippers that had failed. The dress zippers sewn in at Tanana were now useless having soon failed, which we knew would happen. The bugs are bad in the lower river and without netting we would be in trouble. With that thought I fell into a fitful sleep.

06:00 I left the tent and stood in a cold rain. The wind had a sharp edge to it, and whispered of colder days to come. Skeins of wild geese by the hundreds flew, with raucous chatter, over Turtle Island calling loudly to their leaders to set course for the warmer Southland. I stood alone near our tent and gazed at the storm-tormented sky then returned to the tent for more sleep.

07:00 Ken had enough. She dressed and left the tent for coffee. The wind had wrecked our weather fly, so she hid with the Coleman in the lea of a large spruce stump, a real drifter. The coffee she produced in this makeshift shelter was hot and good. More geese flew over head.

Kenny shouted, "Say 'hello' to Mr. Peepers on your way over Maryland." Mr. Peepers was our big Emden goose who couldn't get two feet off the ground. The Canadas looked so majestic in the sky; we looked so forlorn on this island standing in the rain drinking coffee.

Morning was spent repairing our storm-washed and wrecked camp. At eleven-thirty, Neill, Jim and I took binoculars and walked up the island for a look at Cement Hill's headland and the river beyond, or what we could see of it. The wind had abated, and the seas were flatter. We figured we could make the weather point off Cement Hill safely. We hurried back to camp, packed, and at 12:10 we were off down river.

Things went well. We cleared the island and Cement Hill's cliffs nicely. We passed Carlos Island, Paradise, Dividing Point and the double mouthed Koserefski River as thousands of wild geese flew overhead tumbling, wheeling and gabbling about the good weather to come. Holy Cross Hills stood majestically by and watched our passage. By 18:00, we headed for the sandbar on the east end of Walker Slough, having covered twenty-four miles since noon. Our progress was better, but we knew we would be faced with other days of storm during which we would be weather bound as we continued toward St. Mary's, one hundred and eighty miles to the west.

We pulled our canoes to dry land on the point of Walker Slough and the Yukon. Great piles of dry driftwood lay along the high water line like a long fence. We soon had a large fire burning and a snug camp set. Supper was followed by bottomless cups of hot Russian tea and good conversation. It was a relief to be on dry land and off Turtle Island. The whole world looked better from our camp on Walker Slough, especially with the prospect of entering Holy Cross in the morning. We talked again about leaving the river at Holy Cross. Once we reached the village, we would have to make a decision that would either see the end of our Yukon River trip, or would send us by paddles on to St. Mary's.

August 21st started in fine fashion. We were up early, did our chores, packed out and paddled down Walker Slough to Holy Cross, arriving at the landing at 10:00 sharp. We left Jim to watch the boats. Ken, Neill and I walked to the village to look things over and gather information relating to the lower river and weather conditions that we might expect in late August.

We met Carol Hesselman and recognized her immediately as one of the young ladies we had met in a canoe north of Forty Mile, Yukon Territory, some weeks earlier. She turned out to be the principle of Holy Cross School. Carol had canoed the lower Yukon several years ago and had nothing kind to say about the south and west winds one could expect to encounter on the river in late August.

We looked up Pete Turner, agent for Air Wein. We wanted cost and flight information between Holy Cross and Fairbanks. Pete was unable to help us but suggested we await the arrival of the 12:00 bush flight and question the pilot about the possibility of flying our boats and crew to civilization. This sounded like a good idea, so we determined to walk to the airstrip and wait for the plane to arrive.

Having time to kill, we visited the grocery store owned and operated by Betty Johnson. Mrs. Johnson opened the door for us during her lunch hour and allowed us to shop. The river villagers all closed their businesses during the lunch hour, but were always willing to help drifters and travelers who happened by during that time. Betty listened to the account of our trip on the river, and then provided information on the weather from her short wave radio – it predicted continuing storms and extreme south and west winds.

We wanted information on Sea Air, but found no agent. We knew Sea Air had its headquarters in Bethel, but we could not contact them. The satellite telephone system for Holy Cross had

been out of order for over a week and repair was not yet scheduled. Pete Turner, and later, the pilot of the bush plane, told us
that Sea Air had an Otter that could handle our canoes and gear
and enable us to fly to Bethel where we could purchase passage
to Anchorage. The pilot tried to use his radio to reach Bethel but
was unable to make contact with the Bethel air base. Once again,
we were stuck without an answer. We were told by a young Indian that Kathy Chase had a short wave radio in her home and
she would be happy to help us contact Bethel or Fairbanks. We
listened to his directions and located the Chase residence only to
find the door locked. Miss Chase was in Adak.

     Ken, seized with our problem, set off for Holy Cross School.
She contacted our river friend Carol Hesselman to ask her for
help. The school had a short wave radio, which was used to
communicate with the large school district, and could be used to
call Bethel air base. Communication problems in Holy Cross
might just be solved.

     Carol called every hour, but atmospherics prevented contact
with Bethel, Fairbanks, or anywhere in Alaska until 16:30. At
that hour, Carol made contact with Fairbanks, who relayed the
information to Bethel. Thanks to Carol, we learned that the Sea
Air Otter had been wrecked, but Bethel Sea Air was scheduled to
fly a small Beaver to Holy Cross the following day. It would
arrive about 15:30. We would wait and talk to the pilot who, we
hoped, would have information about flights out that we could
take.

     17:00 we returned to Jim and the boats, and paddled slowly
down Walker Slough to a fine sandbar and made camp for the
night. Ken pulled the cork on a frustrating day by reaching in her
snake's hole and producing a pint of Wild Turkey she had set
aside to celebrate the end of our journey. It was the first real
drink we had had in several weeks, and it sure changed the com-
plexion of the day. Next, we ate a real supper and figured the
world was reasonable. With that thought we said goodnight.

     During the night of August 21st a high moved into Holy Cross
quadrant. At 03:00 I arose and left the tent to check things in

general. The sky was clear and a thing of beauty. Stars shone like headlights in the blue velvet of the heavens. I had not seen a sky so clear and bright since my young years of seagoing. I stood awe struck by the brilliance of the sky, viewing Polaris, The Seven Sisters, *Castor* and *Pollux*, and other constellations I had often used as a young man at sea for locating our ship's position.

Ursa Major hung overhead like a big dipper put there by some huge giant for his use. It was obvious why Alaska made the Big Dipper on a royal blue background their State flag. At latitude 62° North, the August sky, when clear, is a sight that one can never forget. The nearness of these first magnitude stars makes a lasting impression. I returned to the tent and sleep.

At 06:00 I slowly opened one eye. I did not have to get up. At 08:45 I barely managed to escape the clutches of my sleeping bag. When I was finally upright, I noted the day was bright and clean with a smart breeze from the northeast. What a day! We ate breakfast feeling great. At 10:00 Jim, Neill and I set out to find the airstrip. We walked across country through alders and short sloughs that barred our path, and had to be worked around. We should have stuck to the sand trail. We were on the strip at 11:30 when a small Beaver landed. The plane belonged to Adak Flying Service. We talked to the pilot about the possibility of moving our boats, gear, and ourselves to Amiak, where we knew we could get jet service to Fairbanks. Amiak is twenty minutes distance by air from Holy Cross.

The pilot estimated the weight of our equipment, then informed us a Beaver would be too small to haul it. He said Adak Flying Service had an Otter, which he thought had been repaired, that might accommodate us. With that, he departed for Amiak to discuss the matter with his company, saying he would return later in the afternoon with the information. We returned to camp where Ken was keeping the watch.

At 12:30 hours Neill, Ken and I returned to Holy Cross. Ken wanted to shop at Mrs. Johnson's grocery. I wanted to settle the business of our departure if it were possible to do so. We all knew we were killing time, and a strong possibility existed we would have to continue on down river in spite of the weather if we wanted to return our canoes to civilization.

Arriving in the village, Neill and I talked to Pete Turner and rode to the airstrip with him and his wife. The Adak pilot had returned and departed. His information was not helpful. He had mistakenly thought our canoes were heavy freight canoes, the kind used on the Yukon that are powered by heavy-duty outboard motors. The Otter could not carry them. Little did he know we were riding eighteen foot wood and canvas Old Towns powered by paddles. We finally caught up with the pilot in the afternoon on one of his freight runs and I explained our boats to him. They were eighteen foot canoes with a three foot beam and a one and a half foot keel depth. They weighed approximately one hundred pounds empty and wet. Again, he departed to check and recheck the capability of the Otter. Neill and I sat on the empty airstrip and waited until 15:30, when three small planes arrived. They were from Adak Flying Service, Sea Air, and Amiak Charter. Our young pilot had re-measured the Otter and found it would not do. Our boats were too long. We talked to the other pilots. Sea Air had a Caribou that could do the job, but it had been smashed on landing and would not be back in service for several weeks. Amiak had a float plane but it too was down for a week for maintenance. In short, we bombed out and it was still one hundred and eighty miles to St. Mary's. Pete Turner stopped his truck as we stood by the roadside. He wanted to know if we had any luck. When we told him no he shrugged and gave us a lift to the village.

We found Ken at the Johnson store talking to Betty Johnson. They were talking about the river and things in Holy Cross. She was the representative for the Adak school district, the most extensive district in the American school system. Betty was Athabascan and Russian. She was related to the Deacons in Grayling. Her Mother, Mrs. Demientioff, had a fish camp on Tabernacle Mountain, and she asked us to stop by for a visit with her. We met her sister, Alice Nerby, who had come from Bethel for a summer visit with her Mother and Betty. Alice had arrived by bush plane from Bethel via Amiak. She lived in Bethel, was married, and had three children. Her husband, a merchant, was home keeping the store.

We bought our supplies. Mrs. Johnson gave Ken a package of fresh smoked salmon, fresh garden vegetables from her garden, and then drove us back to a place near our boats. Thanks to Betty, supper was superb. We ate the turnips and carrots raw, and Ken cooked the potatoes. We knew as we sat around our fire that tomorrow would see us back at the paddles facing the headwind and weather. The pleasure of three days in Holy Cross had revived our spirits and strength. We said goodbye to Betty, and somehow, it was not so far to St.Mary's.

On the 23rd of August, our 68th day on the river, dawn came on silent feet, and with its arrival one of the most beautiful days of late summer was born. At 06:00 I left the tent to be greeted by the sun, no wind and nature in her finest. The air was cool but clear and heavy night dew was in evidence on all things. Breakfast was hot and good. We decamped and left Walker Slough.

Near the south end of the Slough, Ken spotted a red fox feeding on a small dead black bear someone had shot. We paused and watched from the canoes until Mr. Red noticed us and fled into the alders.

New names came to our attention as we worked our way down the Yukon. We canoed past Salmon Island, Horse Island and Big Bend Slough; and they became part of our river knowledge. A motor boat passed us with the occupants yelling, "Halloo, we'll see you at Tabernacle Mountain." It was Alice Nerby on her way to her mother's fish camp.

The Paimuit Hills rose before the bows of *Castor* and *Pollux*, as did Tabernacle Mountain, and there stood Mrs. Demientieff with Alice Nerby waving and "Hallooing" at us, making sure we would not miss their camp. We were immediately invited to the small log structure for tea, homemade bread, cookies, and plenty of smoked silver salmon.

Mrs. Demientieff, Carl Taylor, Alice Nerby, and Neill Prew at Mrs. D's fish camp on Tabernacle Mountain. She and Alice had us to 'Tea,' where they served smoked salmon strips, homemade bread, and cookies.

After tea, Mrs. Demientieff showed us around her fish camp. Hanging in the smokehouse were over five hundred king and silver salmon which she had prepared and hung without help. She smoked these fish for sale and personal use. During the winter months, she repaired the fishnets, made leatherwork such as moccasins, and tatted lace alter cloths for the Holy Cross Catholic Church.

We walked to the foot of Tabernacle Mountain to look at the shrine ninety feet up at the top of the bluff. Alice explained, "The original Church built by my father in Holy Cross burned, and they pushed it down the bank of the river. Mother climbed on the roof, removed the steeple, and brought it here. She also took the red cedar statue of the Virgin Mary, which he had carved. Berry stains gave it the colors to make it look real. Mother placed colorful plastic flowers around the foundation."

Mrs. Demientieff and Ken climbed Tabernacle Mountain to the Catholic shrine she had built in her husband's memory. We watched in awe at the two climbers. Mrs. Demientieff , 84 years old, beat Ken to the top. Ken said it was because she knew where the toeholds were.

Mrs. Demientieff's shrine in memory of her husband. Ken and Mrs. D climbed eighty feet straight up the cliff side to get this picture.

Alice continued, "Mother was brought up in the Catholic Mission. One day a Russian seaman came by and asked the Mother Superior if she would allow one of her orphans to marry him. Mother Superior called in a young girl anxious to leave the mission. The sailor and girl were eighteen years old. They both agreed to the arrangement. Mother Superior than said, *'Now you may kiss him.'* My mother asked, *'Do you kiss boys too?'* Mother Superior answered, *'You may as well go on and kiss him. Tomor-*

row you will be his Mama.' That was 1914. Mother had four children. After her husband died, she never remarried."

We visited for an hour then said goodbye. Mrs. Demientieff and Alice gave us five pounds of smoked silver salmon, then serenaded us with a Russian sea chantey as we bent to our paddles.

By 13:30 we were in Summer Slough north of Great Paimuit Island. We paused for a quick snack of smoked fish, and had just set out once again when we heard a bear growl on the island. Ken spotted a sow and three small cubes eating fish on the shore. That old bear had her hands full with three offspring, and her disposition left much to be desired. We were glad to be on the other side of the river from her. I thought that probably an old boar was trying to eat one of her cubs. We heard, but never saw a second one.

We passed the village of Paimuit at 14:00, and traveled west seven miles before landing on a small sandbar where we camped. Our effort today saw us complete thirty-five miles, which is a reasonable run and can be easily accomplished, weather permitting. We now had one hundred and forty-five miles to St. Mary's. These would be bug-ridden miles, in that we were sixty-five feet above sea level and surrounded by tundra and no-see-ums. Now we could use the wind – at least a little breeze to swish the bugs away. Absent this, we retired to our tents praying for good weather tomorrow.

August 24th dawned bright and still. The sky held salmon tinted clouds and rays of golden sunlight. The hour 06:00. We listened to, and were enchanted by the siren song of Alaska's Indian Summer. We talked of our remaining days on the Yukon. We knew they would be the most tiring of our trip; and, they were passing too slowly with the continuous storms that slowed our progress. We ate breakfast, packed, and decamped. With shoes and socks in our positions in the boats, we pulled and pushed our canoes to deep water, boarded with wet muddy feet and set off down river.

We took fresh water from a mountain freshet near the west end of the Paimuit Hills, then worked our way west, passing

Tucker's Slough on the starboard hand. We were in wide slow water north of Base Island. These waters were full of darting silver salmon whose beautiful silver sides gleamed as they propelled east into the current of the Yukon bound for some stream of their birth to spawn and die, completing another life-cycle in the evolution of things. A wise old seagull knew their history, and quietly floated on the current near the bloated remains of a salmon who had already met its fate. The gull was enjoying a feast, and in all probability reflecting on others yet to come.

Pearl Island, about five miles in length, hosts the Yukon along its high cut banks and serves as home for the thousands of wild geese in its marshes. We were two-thirds of our way along the north side of this hound's head of an island when the wind from nowhere struck like a viper. The west wind blowing over the Illivit Mountains battered our boats and the river. We ran for shelter under the high banks as the river writhed in torment. The sound was one of agony and the scene one of fury. We hid from the storm for about fifteen minutes then carefully worked our way toward a sandbar about two miles more as our day disintegrated into violent wind and rain. We pulled our boats and made camp realizing all too well we would reach our destination, not on our terms, but on those of the Yukon and its fickle weather.

A quick look at the maps pointed to the fact that we were now one hundred, twenty-nine miles from St. Mary's. That was some consolation. Standing around our campfire, watching the wind torture the river, we noted the bugs were not a real problem. The wind, land, and low temperature kept them down. It was not because of our Jansport tents. Yesterday, our last nylon zipper began to act up. This morning it broke. Now all three door zippers had failed. Ken fixed the problem. She lashed out at our tent with needle and thread and sewed herself in. Then she split the bug screen on the window end away from the door and that became our entrance and exit. All we had to do was turn the outer shell end for end. Three cheers for Ken. Now, I wonder what she can do about the wind? And what will her answer be if our last sick zipper fails?

When I awoke at 04:30 and looked out the tent, I knew day seventy would be wind bound. The west was ashen with long, black dissipated wind streaks across the horizon. Rain fell as the wind tugged and tore at our weather fly and tents, causing the nylon to luff, flap and chatter.

Last evening we had two visitors who were camped on the bar southeast of us. The one chap was Indian, and the second Russian and Eskimo. His name was Wilfred Stevens from St. Mary's. The Indian was from Pilot Station. Both were on the bar to cut dry spruce logs for a new cabin that Stevens was building at St. Mary's. There were no logs in the tundra country, so logs had to be cut far up river and floated to the location of the tundra cabin site. Stevens said he was cutting thirty-foot logs to raft to St. Mary's, where his six brothers would help him construct his cabin. He hoped to have his cabin completed before the onset of hard winter. Ken noticed he was wearing a shiny, new wedding band.

During their brief visit we talked of the wind and river. Their picture, a dismal one, held little hope for a break in our wind pattern. It was too late in the season for weather breaks. To complicate matters, both Stevens and the Indian threw a fog-and-rain mix, with quick arctic storms accompanied by heavy seas, into the equation. The river becomes slow and wide with a myriad of sloughs and backwaters as it reaches for the sea. It became clear that in late August, the lower Yukon was no place for canoes, especially with the possibility of sudden storms on a wide open, cold body of water. As both men talked, I silently reviewed our situation. It was neither bad nor good. We were slowly but surely wearing the miles away when we were able to paddle, but one by one our weather bound days during which we could make no progress were counting toward the eventual score of freeze up.

After our friends departed, we talked about the intelligence we had received. We considered alternatives. Roughly, they amounted to reaching Russian Mission within the next two days, weather permitting, and attempting to break our trip there. That approach depended, of course, on the availability of a bush plane large enough to fly our canoes and gear to St. Mary's and commercial transportation.

Our second approach would be to hire an Indian with a large riverboat to transport us and our equipment to St. Mary's. Either type of transportation would solve our problem and eliminate the need to push two eighteen foot canoes one hundred ten miles into the face of quick storms from Norton Sound and the Bering Sea. And at this moment, as the wind ripped at the tents and toyed with the rigging, either solution would be fully acceptable.

The third alternative, and least attractive, involved reaching Russian Mission twenty miles distant to the west, and purchasing sufficient supplies to carry us through more weather bound days and travel days to see us arrive at our hoped for destination Andrefsky, the Russian name for St. Mary's. To reflect on the above did little good. In the bush the word is "survive." To do so in small boats involves a lot of waiting, and waiting when subarctic weather is involved is tough, but safe, and well worth it.

I crawled into the tent to write. Outside, the wind yawed and flawed and a light rain tapped on the tent. Neill and Jim stood by a warming fire, and Ken was carving a cane from a spruce root. Soon she will serve hot tea and I will join them. So – we wait and scan a dismal sky for hints of weather change that would allow onward river travel. The slow erosion of the day made Russian tea and an early supper sound like a good idea. We stood around a roaring fire until 20:30 and watched as wind beat the Yukon to a lather. One by one, we said good night and retired.

All through the night, the wind sobbed and moaned and tore at our tents and camp. Rain – light, heavy and toward dawn a drizzle – pelted our sandbar and beat weird cadences on our tents while the Yukon raged at the tormenting wind and beat violently at the shore. It was a night of fearful sounds that set one's imagination off on acute tangents and allowed one to conjure up fantastic mental pictures of the subarctic storm that engulfed us.

Toward dawn, I left the tent to see first hand what morning held. I was conscious of the dampness that permeated everything. A light rain was falling, or better stated, was being driven by a gusty wind. We were still weather bound. I returned to the tent. Once inside, I realized Ken had slipped out behind me, so I left the door for her to pin shut. Our outer zipper no longer worked. Ken returned, fastened the flap with appropriate comments, mentioned the weather in like terms and settled in her sleeping bag.

At 07:00 Jim had the fire going. Neill was busy collecting rainwater from our weather fly, which was partially down as a result of the wind. Nothing moved. The clouds rolled and revealed strings of wild geese and marsh ducks flying high in the wind and complaining bitterly about the storm. We could not help but agree with their complaints. Ken had breakfast ready. We stood around the fire and ate in silence. We watched the wind beat on our fire and listened as the fire raged at the wind and threw sparks in wild abandon toward an angry Yukon. We knew we would have to wait a weather change.

The day passed slowly. We tended our fire, dumped water from *Castor* and *Pollux*, napped, wrote and read. Ken checked the food supply – three days rations were left. We cleaned out the last jar of peanut butter for lunch. We had eaten our way through 23 pounds. 19:00 Jim took the shotgun and walked up the bar to try his luck. Ken prepared supper and we three ate. Jim could eat when he returned. While Ken was preparing supper, our neighbors came by. They had logged all day. Wilfred Stevens said he had just killed a wild goose. He invited me to their camp to eat goose meat with them, but I begged off telling them my supper was waiting. At 20:00, we crawled into our tents to escape the wind and bugs. Perhaps tomorrow the wind would be still and let us continue down river.

Heavy wind and squalls plagued us throughout the night, slashing and punishing our camp and the dark world. 03:00 I checked the sky for signs of relief. There were none. I returned to my sleeping bag. At 06:00 rain was still falling. I stayed in the tent until I heard Neill and Jim up. I joined them and together we started the morning fire. Ken, under the weather fly making coffee, left her task to help us. Breakfast was soon over. We dumped the boats and watched for a weather change.

By 09:30 we had enough of waiting. We packed our gear and made ready to depart. At 10:15, we waded through cold mud in bare feet and were afloat on a rather turbulent Yukon. We washed the mud from our feet and dressed them. We cleared our bar by dint of hard labor, and passed Tucker's Slough in a good bounce. The wind from the west beat on us without mercy, hurtling one line squall after another at our laboring canoes. We were cold and wet.

Baldhead Mountain, Mount Ewaklalik at 1,860 feet, Dog Fish Mountain, and Tucker's Fish Camp passed by to starboard. Cottonwood Point lay on the port hand. We bounced, splashed, and slopped our way west down an angry river pausing once for lunch and a quick fire for warmth. By 16:00, we were north and east of Johnson Island on a point of land. We debated going on, but finally settled and made camp. We had risked the Yukon, which was not real bright, and had been rewarded with eleven miles of progress. It took five hours work amid wind, squalls and heavy seas. I paused to figure the speed we were making over the ground and determined it to be about 3mph. This meant the head wind cut by half the speed of our canoes on a 6mph current.

We checked the map and realized that tomorrow, with any break in the weather, we could make Russian Mission. With that in mind we all retired for the night.

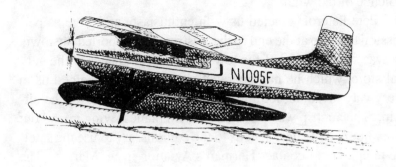

CHAPTER XI
Russian Mission, Air Borne, and Homeward

On the 28th of August, our log indicated we had spent seventy-three days and worked our way through ninety-one maps and sixty-one camps on the Yukon. We faced another morning of wind, rain and bad weather. The three cardinal sins of canoeing stayed with us through the night and early morning. We lay in our tents and listened to the wind tear at our shelter and drive rain like shot into the fabric. By 07:00 we crawled out to face the day, by 09:30 the storm abated and we packed. At 10:00 we were on a wide windswept river, bound for Johnson Island, which we passed at 10:45. The sea was choppy and the going rough.

At 12:00, we ate lunch in the sunshine on Barefaced Bluff Point across from the south end of Arctic Island. Back on the river, we paddled through our second squall of the day. Rounding Barefaced Bluff, we ran into a wicked storm that lasted long enough to soak us. We crossed a wide bend in the river, rounded a second high bluff, pounding and slopping our way into Russian Mission.

We landed at 13:45. Our total time on the river was three hours and ten minutes, during which we covered nine miles with rain squalls every three miles. The weather had gone from bad to rotten. It was good to be on dry ground and protected from the violence of the wind.

Pete Peteroff greeted us with enthusiasm and gave us permission to camp at the end of the airstrip that supported the town. He was sole member of the town council and owner of the general store, which he had operated since 1963. He helped us in every way he could, letting us set camp near the end of the airstrip. The airstrip was a busy one, with planes flying in and out every hour or so. Pete sent us to the commissary to use the satellite telephone to contact Herman's Aviation in St. Mary's. The Commissary, built at the highest point in the village, was easily protected from pilfering. It contained hundreds of cases of rifle ammunition of all calibers, at least a hundred cases of canned milk, and cartons of rice. Winter clothing, mostly military issue, lay unused and mildewing on shelves built around the walls of the building. We found the phone on the back wall and talked with Stan Herman. He had a 185 on floats, and he could fly our two canoes and gear to Saint Mary's about midday August 29th. He would send a second plane in for us.

Russian Mission, where we ended our journey. The oil cans strewn around on the ground are called Alaskan Cactus. They are ubiquitous in Alaska.

Russian Mission dates back to the days of Russian owner-ship of Alaska. Its population was one hundred and fifty, mostly Eskimos. The Eskimos were as friendly as the rest of the villag-ers we had met on our canoe trip. They stopped to talk with us about our trip and experiences on the river. One tiny "Lady," speaking to all of us, with her back to Ken and her eyes on Jim, *"I love Russian Mission — everyone love Russian Mission — everyone come m'house – m'house over there..."* She pointed toward her house and continued, *"We drink a little.... love a little..."* touching Jim's arm, *"Y' wanna come m'house?"* Neill poked Jim in the back. Jim turned red-faced and I was laughing inside. At that moment Harold Mitchell walked into camp and introduced himself.

Harold supervised the carpenters for the Tate Corporation that was building twenty-seven new homes in Russian Mission at a cost of $88,000 each. They were three and four bedroom, oil-heated houses located on a hill behind the old Russian Ortho-dox Church that dated from the days of Russian ownership. The government planned to spend five million dollars installing a sewer and water system and a new airstrip. The pending devel-opment, coupled with oil heat in the houses, should do much to bring Russian Mission close to the twentieth century.

The old ways of the Eskimo were being eliminated. They would no longer have to walk to the riverbank on icy mornings to cut their small bucket of driftwood for their fires. Eskimos never cut firewood in the summer for winter use, nor do they stack extra wood near their homes. The Yukon River carries the trees during the spring run off. As the fallen trees float down river, the Eskimos, in their outboard motor boats, tow them to the bank. The trees become the property of each man's haul to be cut for his winter fuel.

The Skidoo, or snow mobile, had replaced the dog teams. The dogs, now a status symbol and secondary transportation, were kept on chains along the bank of the river. Dogs found running loose were shot, as they were dangerous to the women and chil-dren.

These visits would have continued throughout the evening
had not the weather threatened. The sky turned black around
19:00 hours and the usual happened. It rained. We said goodbye
to the balance of the day and retired to the comfort of our tents.

On the morning of the 29th of August, Ken and I awakened
with no thought of the weather. No paddles today. We poked
Neill from his tent, and we three walked to the Tate Corp.
cookhouse where we met Bruce Letho of Seattle, Washington.
Bruce was Chef for Tate Construction. We talked with Bruce
and enjoyed the warmth of the cookhouse and hot coffee. We
also enjoyed the use of indoor toilets that Bruce gave us permission to use. Outside it rained and Jim slept on in his tent.

At 13:00 we walked back to Tate's and enjoyed some left-
over chicken noodle soup. 13:45 Stan Herman arrived in his
185. We watched as he loaded our canoes. Ken took pictures as
he taxied out into the river and became air borne. Our boats
would soon be in Saint Mary's. At 16:30 hours, Ed Landis arrived in a Cessna Air Coupe. We loaded our gear and ourselves
into his plane with the assistance of our tiny "Lady" who wished
to help us. We gave her our buckets and other sundry gear. She
waved good-by with a grin on her face, happy for the small to-
kens of friendship.

The river trip was over for us. The cold was setting down;
the nights were getting long. We had canoed over eighteen hundred miles from an altitude of 2,060 feet in Lake Laberge to 25
feet above sea level in Russian Mission. We had met the
Athabascan and the Eskimo. We paddled through the Rockies,
the land of spruce and poplar to the tundra, the land of swamp
and muskeg. We paddled through the largest waterfowl breeding
grounds in North America. We saw much wild game, met many
friends, fought the wind and rain as relentlessly as the wind and
rain fought us.

It was a river full of friends *"we'll see someplace."*

EPILOGUE

Returning to Whitehorse was a Homeric epic of confusion, misdirection, false starts, and a hair-raising drive down the muddy Alaska Highway.

We were twenty minutes out of Saint Mary's when Ed radioed the airfield. A cargo jet, unscheduled, was due to return to Anchorage empty. We wanted to know if they would fly our boats from Saint Mary's to Anchorage. The field advised that we would have to talk to the pilot. We arrived at 17:30 and met Howard M. Pierce, Field Manager. Howard told us the cost to fly our boats to Anchorage on Wien Air Alaska would be sixteen hundred dollars. Forget that!

Finally, N-6119-C landed with our canoes. The plane, property of Northern Air Cargo, was flown by Jerry Vink. I talked to Jerry and he placed a call to his office in Anchorage. His office did not object to flying our boats and gear out, and he would be glad to help us. Jerry took our canoes and gear to Anchorage for one hundred dollars – fifty dollars a boat. The gods of good fortune smiled on us. I then chartered Ed Landis to fly us on to Bethel where we caught Wien Air Flight number sixteen to Anchorage. We arrived there at 23:30 and found lodging at the Ramada Inn. Hot showers were a thing sent from heaven. Our next stop was the lounge, where we enjoyed several good drinks. A hot dinner and, finally, real beds ended our day. No more sleeping bags for us this summer.

On the 30th of August, we awakened to indoor quiet; no sound of wind or rain. We reluctantly left our soft beds for the next best thing. Breakfast of fresh eggs, orange juice, coffee served up by someone else at a table with chairs to sit on. The Ramada surely equaled the luxury of Buckingham Palace.

09:45 we returned to the ordinary and took a cab to the airport, where we began a systematic search for our twins. We found them with our gear at Northern Air Corp Inc. Jerry Vink had delivered them as promised. Now we had to arrange onward transportation to Fairbanks. Maurie Fitzhugh of Northern Air Cargo proved to be the key. Maurie had several suggestions, the first one being Wien Air. That bombed out big time. No service connected Anchorage with the Yukon Territory. My question, "What about flying the canoes to Fairbanks?" "No problem. They will take three pallet spaces." The clerk added, "Each space costs $1,000." A quick addition on one hand figured the total worth of cargo space to move our gear. That caused our respective pancreases to act up.

We promptly forgot Wien Air. By 14:00 we had covered all exits. There was no cheap way out of Anchorage, at least by air. We turned to trucks. We telephoned Linden trucking. Linden would drive our boats and equipment to Fairbanks. We thanked Douglas Hanson of Northwest Freight for that bit of good news. Doug drove Neill and me to the Northern Air Cargo office where we talked to Connie Johnston and Maurie Fitzhugh about Linden. Both Connie and Maurie were pleased, and agreed to handle our gear with Linden and keep us informed regarding the time of pick up at Northern Air Cargo freight yard, if I would give them a call.

Neill and I, satisfied we had things going, returned to the cocktail lounge at the Anchorage Airport to join Ken and Jim who were waiting there with our personal baggage.

About 16:00 my skin felt like the williwaws. I left to call Northern Air Cargo about the boats. Connie answered, "Yes, there was a problem." I groaned. "The Linden truck driver will not accept canoes unless you have them boxed or wrapped." We were once again in the hands of a snake-haired avenging deity. Maurie saved the day.

Northern Air had a job to do in the Brooks Range on August 31st. They would insure delivery of our boats on that date if we could meet the cargo plane at the Cliff Everett's yard in Fairbanks.

Had Connie told me that she would have got a big kiss, Maurie just got a big handshake. I hurried back to the lounge. Seeing my hurried walk, the three lounge lizards stood up ready to go.

"We have to be at the yard at 12:00 hours on the 31st to pick up our boats and gear and pay the pilot." I filled in the rest of the info as we boarded an Alaska Air at 18:00 hours. Landing at Fairbanks at 20:00 hours, we were met by Lorna.

We checked in at the Chena View Hotel. The night was spent talking about our great run of luck in getting off the Yukon with the help of Northern Air Cargo, and particularly Maurie Fitzhugh with his gang of guys and gals who took an interest in us. It reminded us of all those who had helped us get safely down the Yukon River.

August 31st we were up at 06:00, had breakfast, and drove to the Cliff Everett's yard to await our gear, due to arrive at 11:45. While waiting, we called several airline and trucking companies in Fairbanks in an effort to get our gear from Fairbanks to Whitehorse, a distance of six hundred miles. There was no solution to our transportation problem. We could book passage, but we could not move our canoes or equipment. We were told agreements between the Canadian and U.S. Government would not allow small cargo shipments. In short it could not be done with less than a full truckload for delivery.

Lorna saved the day. Lorna had ordered a parka in Whitehorse when they were there to see us off. The store had called about a problem with the fit. Now she needed to go see about it. Why not use their truck to move people, gear and boats down the Alaska Highway to Whitehorse? Our respective problems were solved.

At 14:00 the Northern Air Cargo plane arrived. Everything was in good order. At 15:00 Neill and I built a two by four rack on the truck shell for the boats. We loaded our gear aboard and made ready to travel the next morning. I called the Airline Inn in Whitehorse for reservations the following night.

September 1st we began our journey down the Alaska Highway. We checked out of the Chena at 06:00 and loaded ourselves in the truck, two in the back and three up front. We set out in search of breakfast and gasoline, which we found one hundred twenty-five miles south at The Evergreen Lodge in Delta Junction.

From Delta Junction, we drove to the Alaska–Yukon Territory border where the blacktop petered out and the real Alaska Highway began. Mud ruled the highway with an iron hand. Add permafrost, chuckholes, and rain, and you have a nightmare. And that was where we found ourselves. The temperature, at 38°, kept the truck bed cold for two of us. Heavy drenching rain and gusting winds kept the driver and other two equally miserable. One might say we endured taking turns at all equally miserable positions in the truck for twelve solid hours.

Coming into Haines Junction, the right rear tire began to hiss and slowly deflate. We changed to our spare in the mud and rain. We slipped, slid and bounced our way into Whitehorse, where Airline Inn had beds waiting for us. The time of arrival was 01:00. We had laid six hundred miles of our return journey to rest at The Airline Inn. Don Witunik greeted us. He looked relieved, as he had become uncertain as to whether we would return or not.

On September 2nd, we started at 06:00 to get the car ready for travel. Although we had disconnected the battery in June, we knew it would need a recharge when we returned. The sick truck tire had to be repaired, and the truck needed a bath. We did some last minute shopping, and spent time in the lounge drinking beer and writing cards to friends. The day passed quickly, and at supper we talked of the Alaska Highway and our departure. We made reservations at Watson Lake, two hundred and ninety-eight miles to the south. It would be a long drive due to the road conditions, but we were in a hurry to end our journey. We had been away from home for a long time.

The morning of September 3rd, we said goodbye to our friends at the Airline Inn, filled our car with gasoline at the Whitehorse Service Station, and drove to Rotary Park, where we had launched our canoes on the 17th of June. The Yukon, clear and swift, was higher than it had been in June. She beckoned, but we knew her secrets. We felt no urge to heed her call. Everyone took pictures, and then we said our goodbyes – Lorna and Jim back to Fairbanks, us to the Lower Forties.

The bumper strip on a passing car summed it all up: "We drove the entire length of the Alaska Highway and lived."

ABOUT THE AUTHOR,
The Crew, The Artist, And The Canoes

Carl T. Taylor grew up in Michigan, where canoes and rivers in the Upper were as natural to a boy's education as school. His seagoing career started at age sixteen, when he qualified for a Maritime ticket. He spent two and a half seasons on the Great Lakes, then went into the Navy at the beginning of WWII, where he was the champion boxer of the 5th Destroyer Division. After the war, he entered government service in the CIA. Over the years he canoed many rivers, including the Danube, Mosel, and Lohn in Europe. He and his wife, Kendrick, retired to a farm in Alleghany County, Virginia.

Neill Prew, from Sarasota, Florida accompanied Carl as his bowman on many of the river trips. He took the stern position on *Castor* for the Yukon River trip.

Jim Smith, from Bakersfield, California, brother-in-law of John Taylor, jumped at the chance to be bowman for Neill in *Castor*.

Kendrick Taylor, no stranger to the outdoors, had recently completed a 335-mile horseback ride on the Bicentennial Wagon Train, when she volunteered for the bow position in *Pollux*.

Mary Laur, who provided the book's illustrations, is an artist and printmaker. She maintains her own press and studio in Maryland. Some of the illustrations were based upon photographs taken by Kendrick along the Yukon.

The canoes were named *Castor* and *Pollux* after the twins of Greek mythology. *Castor* was a horseman and *Pollux* was a boxer. Both canoes were Otcas from Old Town. This broad-beamed canoe, which rode seas well because the bow sheared water away from the hull, is now only available from Old Town by special order.

CANOE DIAGRAM

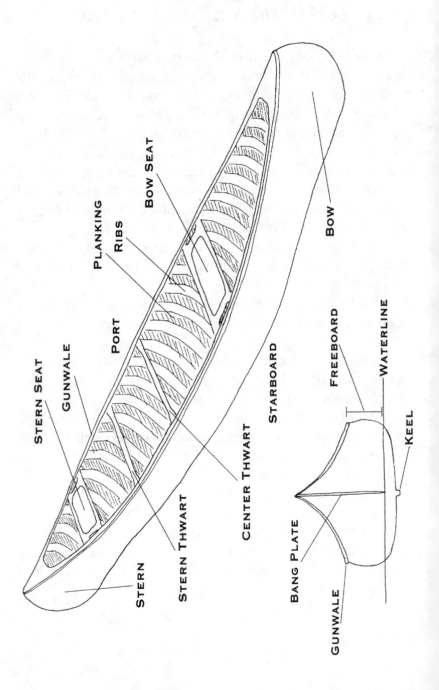

MAP OF ALASKA

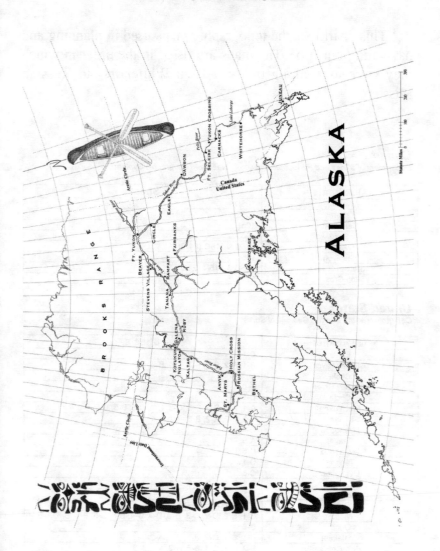

TOPOGRAPHIC MAPS

This chart lists the topographic maps used in planning and navigating our trip. The maps are listed in the order in which they were used along the way from Whitehorse to Russian Mission.

Canada
Department of Mines and Resources, Edition 3, National Topographic System

– Quadrants –	– Sheets –
Whitehorse	105D
Laberge	105E
Carmacks	105I
Snag	105J & 105K
Dawson	116B & 116C (E1/2)
Glenlyon	105L
Stewart River	115O & 115N (E1/2)
Yukon Crossing	115 1/8

United States
Department of the Interior, Geological Survey

– Quadrants –	– Sheets –
Eagle	C-1, D-2
Charley River	A-1, A-2, B-2, B-3, B-4, B-5, B-6, C-6
Circle	C-1
Charley River	D-6
Circle	D-1
Fort Yukon	A-1, A-2, B-2, B-3, C-3, C-4, C-5, B-5, C-6, B-6
Beaver	B-1, B-2, A-2, B-3, A-3, A-4
Livengood	D-4
Beaver	A-5
Livengood	D-5, D-6
Tanana	D-1
Livengood	C-6
Tanana	C-1, B-1, B-2, B-3, A-3, A-4, A-5, A-6
Melozitna	A-1,A-2,A-3
Ruby	D-3,D-4,D-5,C-5,C-6,D-6
Nulato	C-1, C-2, D-2, C-3, D-3, D-4, C-4, D-5, C-5, B-5, B-6, A-6
Ophir	D-6
Unalakeet	D-1, C-1, C-2, B-1, B-2, A-2
Holy Cross	B-2, D-3, C-3, B-3, B-2, A-2, A-3
Russian Mission	D-3,D-4,D-5,D-6,D-7

ORDER FORM

Paddles On The Yukon
1,800 miles in a canoe on the Wildest River in North America

$15.95 for one copy, and order a second for $10.95

Yes,I want to know what it is like to make an extensive canoe trip down one of the world's twenty longest rivers.

Please send one copy pf *Paddles On The Yukon* $15.95
Plus shipping and handling 2.00
____Additional copies for $10.95 each .... _____
Plus shipping and handling -
  $1.00 each additional book .... _____
Virginia residents add 4.5% State Sales Tax .... _____

                     Total Order .... _____

Canadian orders must be accompanied by a postal money order in US funds. Allow three weeks for delivery.

          Name   _____
Shipping Address   _____
    City/State/Zip   _____

Please make check payable to:
Mountain Empire Publications
P.O. Box 480
Clifton Forge, VA 24422-3512

Quantity Discounts Available